P9-DHP-410

BY JOHN MCPHEE

Looking for a Ship
The Control of Nature
Rising from the Plains
Table of Contents
La Place de la Concorde Suisse
In Suspect Terrain
Basin and Range
Giving Good Weight
Coming into the Country
The Survival of the Bark Canoe
Pieces of the Frame
The Curve of Binding Energy
The Deltoid Pumpkin Seed
Encounters with the Archdruid
The Crofter and the Laird
Levels of the Game
A Roomful of Hovings
The Pine Barrens
Oranges
The Headmaster
A Sense of Where You Are

LOOKING FOR A SHIP

LOOKING FOR A SHIP

John McPhee

The Noonday Press

Farrar Straus Giroux

New York

Printed in the United States of America
Published in Canada by Macfarlane Walter & Ross
Designed by Cynthia Krupat
First published in 1990 by Farrar, Straus and Giroux
First published by The Noonday Press in 1991
Library of Congress Cataloging-in-Publication Data
McPhee, John A.
Looking for a ship / John McPhee.—1st ed.
1. Stella Lykes (Ship) 2. Seafaring life. I. Title.
G540.M365 1990 910.4'5—dc20 90-3311

The text of this book originally
appeared in The New Yorker

The engraving on the title page and chapter openings is from the United States Coast Guard licenses to Masters of United States Steam or Motor Vessels of any Gross Tons upon Oceans

For Yolanda

LOOKING FOR A SHIP

Andy was worried about the Ben Sawyer Bridge. He thought of it stuck open, and saw in his mind's eye an unending line of stifled cars, his own among them. If his neurons seemed hyperactive, they had some reason to be. On the other hand, how often did this drawbridge get stuck? Once a year? Three times every two years? Whatever the statistics might be, they would make no difference to Andy. The drawbridge had stuck open one afternoon with him on the wrong side, and the delay was so prolonged that he checked into a motel and caught up on sleep. On that day, he wasn't going anywhere important. On this day, he allowed a minimum of three hours to complete a journey of thirty minutes. He was looking for a ship.

In Andy's wallet was a National Shipping Card that had been stamped in Boston ten and a half months before, registering under his name, George Anderson Chase, the date, the hour, and the minute when he arrived in a union hall after leaving his last ship. The older the card, the better the prospects for a new job. If the card were to go twelve months unused, it would roll over—lose all seniority, and begin again. Meanwhile strongly competitive, it had all but reached the status of a killer card. In the evolving decline of the United States Merchant Marine, qualified people seeking work so greatly outnumbered the jobs there were to fill that you almost had to hold a killer card or your chances were slim for shipping out. You went to a union hall, presented the card in person at a job call, and if someone tossed in an older card you stayed on the beach. From his home, in Maine, Andy had come to Charleston this time because he thought that shipping cards deadlier than his would be more numerous in Boston or New York. On sheer speculation, I joined him, our idea being that when he got himself a ship he would ask the shipping company if I could go along on the voyage as a P.A.C.—Person in Addition to Crew. Andy said, "I probably have a better chance out of Charleston. Fewer people. Less competition. A fairly steady stream of ships." Besides, he had a place to stay. His wife's mother lived on an island whose connection to the mainland was the Ben Sawyer Bridge.

We had no idea where we would be going, if anywhere. We had gear for cool weather and gear for the tropics. Looking for a ship, Andy had once spent two months fruitlessly hanging around the union hall in Charleston. He had put in many weeks in New York with the same result. He once went as far as Puerto Rico. He spent two weeks there going to the hall. He got no ship. He tried Charleston on his way home, and with great luck got a ship in two days. The ship he got in Charleston was called the Puerto Rican. He was on it four months, sailing as third mate, coastwise. A chemical tanker, it blew up, out of San Francisco, on a later voyage. It broke in half.

I had known Andy for several years. I had been to his home in Maine. I had accompanied him to the New York hall of the International Organization of Masters, Mates, and Pilots. The New York hall is in Jersey City. On the PATH train, Andy said, "The union halls are not really halls. They're like dentists' offices." This one was a room on the east side of the fifteenth floor of a fairly new building at 26 Journal Square. The view of Manhattan was unimpeded from the midtown skyline to the towers of world trade. Andy was just checking out New York. His card was only thirty days old, and he was taking the long chance of finding a short trip that no one else in his category would want. By union rules, he could not do his checking by telephone. If he called the hall, the dispatcher would not tell him who was competing for what. One of the mariners in the hall was a friend of Andy's named Bryan Thomas, who explained to me, "You might trust a friend to check out a hall for you, but what friend? Almost anyone would tell you not to bother coming, no matter what the work situation might be." He went on to say that he had been surprised as he shook my hand, because "there seemed to be some sincerity" in the warmth of my hello. Andy told him that I was no threat.

Thomas said, "There is so much hunger for work that

no one is happy to see anybody else. We are a brotherhood, so we hate each other."

Andy said, "Nobody ever does anybody a favor. You can't beg a job off of somebody. It just isn't done."

The New York hall was about the size of a high-school classroom, and an interior window separated it from a small office. At one-thirty, the time of the job call, action would take place at the window. Job sheets, if any, would be posted on a corkboard. Meanwhile, there was a clipboard with a sheaf of papers headed "OFFSHORE JOBS," showing positions that had been picked up in recent weeks and the age of the cards that had won them. Some of the runs were "Coastwise," "Far East," "South America," "N. Europe," "R/World," "W. Africa," "Caribbean," "Med," "Panama." Andy said, "South America is the romance run—beautiful women, beautiful ports." Andy had never been to South America. To make unexpected replacements, owners will fly people to foreign ports. In extremes, they have used the Concorde. Andy once turned up for a job call at the New York hall and that night was on a flight to Athens. On each offshore-job sheet was a "Reason" column, explaining why the job had come open: "LOA" (leave of absence), "Quit," "Fired." One sheet had called for a mariner to fly off at once on Iberia to Gibraltar. "Rotary" was the reason. He replaced someone whose hundred and twenty days were up—the maximum sea time allowed by the union, in the interest of rationing available work.

As one-thirty neared, more than thirty mates were

fanned out around the office door like fish at the mouth of a tributary stream. They wore nylon jackets, down vests, rubber-soled moccasins, bluejeans, cotton-flannel shirts, fatigue jackets, trenchcoats, sweaters. Nobody looked nautical. Two were in suits and ties. This could have been any carpenters' or plumbers' union hall. Add cowboy boots and it could have been a union hall in Fairbanks at the fading end of the pipeline boom.

"The majority don't tell you what they do in their other lives," Andy said. He had shipped out with restaurateurs, real-estate entrepreneurs, and a lot of people who, in the proximity of fresh water, "just go fishing." The cook on one of Andy's ships was a male stripper. Andy had shipped out with an engine-room wiper in his sixties who called his broker from every port. Andy had shipped out with a sax player who had lost two fingers when they became caught between a mooring line and a capstan. For unrelated reasons, he was known as Goldfinger.

The dispatcher came to the window. The thirty-odd faces lifted in attention. Loudly, the dispatcher said, "Nothing on the offshore," and he read the particulars of four night-mate jobs—eight-hour relief work on docked ships—in Port Elizabeth and Howland Hook. That was it. That was the work available for all those mates. They showed no surprise and quickly dispersed. Sometimes, if you hang around a union hall after all the other people have left, a desperate last-minute call will come in, and if you want the job you can have it. "You dash down and join the ship,"

Andy said. "But that is very rare." Shipping out that way is known as "a pierhead jump." On this day, no one was jumping.

Andy was sixteen when he dropped out of school and first went to sea. Eventually, he finished school but intended not to go to college. After another year at sea, however, he enrolled at Maine Maritime Academy, in Castine, and in 1979 he became a Merchant Marine licensed officer, a third mate. Before long, he was hanging around New Orleans and New York, a month each, attending daily job calls. In those days, jobs were a little more plentiful, but for someone that green there was no ship. Becoming frantic, he tried Boston, the anachronist center of commerce, where he found a square-rigger, a barkentine, casting off to do whale research in the Caribbean. She was called Regina Maris. He shipped out under sail.

The irony of Andy's career is this: as his sea time accumulated and his status in the union improved, his increasing potentiality as a job seeker was largely offset by a decreasing number of jobs, as Chapter 10 started coming to the end for the United States Merchant Marine. After three weeks in New York one spring, he got a job on a container ship called Sea-Land Oakland that shuttled between Rotterdam and the Persian Gulf. The temperature of the Red Sea was ninety-five degrees and the air was over a hundred. In 1983, he had luck in Charleston, where he went to the hall for three weeks and, with a better card than four competitors, became third mate of the LASH Pacifico, a Prudential Lines ship, on which he spent six months and made sixty thousand dollars. He was twenty-eight when he joined the ship. He had been married less than a month before. The sixty thousand dollars was actually a full year's income, because, by terms then set by the union, the six months of work were followed by six of obligatory vacation.

And then another six of utter frustration looking for a ship. He failed to get one in New York, in New Orleans, in Port Everglades, in Charleston. Tension grew within him as the end of a year approached. He had seen a man get a ship with a card that was three hundred and sixty-four days twenty-three hours and fifty-six minutes old. ("He was sweating.") For Andy, the end came without a ship. He still refers funereally to "the day my card rolled over." He needed work so badly that he signed up as an able-bodied seaman on an integrated tug-barge operating between Perth Amboy and Duluth. He was a licensed officer of ocean ships on his way to the Great Lakes as a deckhand on a barge.

To provide jobs of any kind for its increasingly distressed mariners, the Masters, Mates, and Pilots union arranged for five oceangoing tankers to be crewed with union members, right down to the last deckie. Licensed officers accepted jobs as ordinary seamen, able-bodied seamen, and bosuns because they could not get other work. Andy sailed from Providence as an A.B. on the tanker Spray. Later, for many months, he was bosun on the Spray. He was not entirely troubled by this. It gave him a chance to practice marlinspike seamanship—knot tying, wire splicing, rope splicing, rigging. There is an expression in the Merchant

Marine that describes officers who are former deckhands or engine-room wipers and rose to licensed rank not by going to college—not by graduating from one of the seven maritime academies—but by passing examinations after learning on the job. Such people are said to have come up the hawsepipe. Hawsepipes are the apertures in the bows of ships through which the anchor chains clatter. Hawsepipes are the eyes of Yangtze junks. When a big-enough ship is at anchor, a person can climb up one of the chains and make it through the hawsepipe to the fo'c'sle deck. To the question "What academy did you go to?" a licensed officer may answer, "I didn't. I came up the hawsepipe." Andy likes to say that he has been through the hawsepipe, too, but in the wrong direction. As someone who went to an academy, sailed third mate, earned his second mate's license, and then was forced to work as a deckhand, he will tell you that he was "stuffed *down* the hawsepipe."

The United States Merchant Marine, the name of which suggests an assault on a valuable foreign beach, is not, as a good many people seem to think, a branch of military service. It is essentially a collective enterprise of competing private companies, flying the American flag on the sterns of their ships, employing American-citizen crews, and transporting cargoes throughout the world. Sail and steam, the United States grew in rank among nations on the aggressive reach of its Merchant Marine. American merchant ships once numbered in the thousands. The chimerical ship that Andy Chase and I went to look for in Charleston would not be a selection from a field that large.

Diminishing rapidly, the number of American dry-cargo ships was already below two hundred, and there were about as many tankers. Not one commercial vessel was under construction in an American shipyard.

In time of war, the Merchant Marine is a prominent participant. This civilian job—risky enough at any time—becomes exceptionally dangerous. During the Second World War, the percentage of deaths was higher in the Merchant Marine than it was in the Navy or the Army, and was exceeded only by the percentage of deaths in the Marine Corps. Something like eight hundred ships went down and six thousand five hundred sailors died. As prisoners of the Japanese, American merchant mariners were among those who built the bridge on the River Kwai. War, with its all-out sealifts—the Korean Sealift, the Vietnam Sealift—expands the merchant fleet. Afterward, the ships go out of service more rapidly than the sailors, and jobs are hard to come by. The unions close their membership books until numbers level out. By the late nineteen-seventies, the Second World War crowd was gone, and much of the Vietnam crowd. Books opened. There were days when Andy actually felt positive about his choice of career: "Much more young blood coming up now. It's starting to feel as if it's my Merchant Marine. My generation. Our turn has come." In the mid-eighties, "everything slammed shut again" as the United States Merchant Marine was competitively outbid by ships under foreign flags and was reduced to carrying less than five per cent of all oceangoing American cargo. One American company after another entered Chapter 11 with its keel up and its screws in the air. Soon the Soviet merchant fleet was carrying at least ten times as much American cargo as the United States Merchant Marine, in direct trade between the two countries—a multiple that keeps growing through time.

In 1988, the National Maritime Union sold its nine-story building at 346 West Seventeenth Street, Manhattan, which had medical facilities, a gymnasium, a sauna, a restaurant, a theatre, and a school, and—with its porthole windows—suggested an upended ship. The N.M.U., of course, was a sailors' union—the once very powerful organization of the unlicensed—and now it had lost a leveraged sellout, was called M.E.B.A./N.M.U., and had been merged with a branch of the Marine Engineers' Beneficial Association, an organization of engine-room officers. N.M.U. sailors who were looking for ships were reporting to a new address: 404 Lafayette Street, in the saddle of low structures that lie on the loose gravels between the high summits of midtown and Wall Street. The building looks like a warehouse that has seen its last ware. What doorway to use is not clear from the sidewalk and less so if someone is lying in it. Upstairs is a large low room where the bright polish of the maple floor does little to console the N.M.U. sailors for the lost symbol of their lovely hall. The job-call scene is much the same as it is elsewhere for the masters and mates. The board says "Killer Card Date: April 8," or whatever it happens to be. An N.M.U. card accrues seniority for only two hundred and ten days, and then rolls over. Say a car carrier belonging to Central Gulf is the only ship on the board, with two A.B. positions—vacation relief. That's all. And a short run to boot—San Juan. More than forty men are in the hall. Two jobs. It's a lively, noisy room, a hubbub of chatter, many styles of fits-all visored cap, leather jackets, running shoes, flannels, jeans. Any one of those present will know a good many of the others, having sailed with them across the years. While the men wait around to lose out and go home, they argue politics at the shouting level. Each one's picture of the President of the United States seems to be framed entirely by what—as the sailor sees it—the President might do to the Merchant Marine.

The N.M.U. hall in Savannah is a quarter the size of the one in the warehouse in New York—a small freestanding building a few blocks from the Savannah River. You step in off the street and show your killer card. If a sailor doesn't have one, he may be in some difficulty. When I was there one time, Barbara Evans, the dispatcher, said, "Someday I'm going to be a social worker, because that is what I am now." She mentioned sailors who came looking for ships and slept on park benches until they moved to the Inner City Night Shelter. She mentioned a sailor living *under* a house.

The Masters, Mates, and Pilots hall to which Andy and I reported in Charleston was considerably smaller than any other hall I have mentioned: second floor, no windows, three little rooms—an office for a dentist with a hand-me-down drill. It was on Sam Rittenberg Boulevard—an elongate bazaar—and not far from the Truluck Chiropractic

Auto Accident Clinic. By the union's see-through door, a poster said "SHIP AMERICAN, IT COSTS NO MORE." On the first morning there, we looked through the sheaf of bygone jobs and noted the recent destinations: a Lykes Brothers ship to the Mediterranean, a Waterman ship to the Middle East, a Navieras ship to San Juan, a Sea-Land ship to Iceland, a Central Gulf ship to North Europe, a Lykes Brothers ship to the west coast of South America. That, at a glance, was the Charleston pattern, suggesting what might come. Musing over the possibilities, Andy had said that the three most likely were a Sea-Land ship, a Lykes Brothers ship, and a Navieras ship, and that his predilections ran strongly to Lykes Brothers and their run to South America, where he had never been. Least attractive to him was Navieras de Puerto Rico, with its roll-on/roll-off (Ro/Ro) ships—in effect, truck ferries—on a short domestic haul. Aboard a Navieras ship, he said, you would find "a different crowd of people—ones that don't want to go overseas." Not that he could expect to shop for adventure. There had been a time when he thought he would specialize in break-bulk ships with topping lifts and king posts—the classical "stick ship," the freighter with a forest of booms, carrying dry miscellaneous cargo that you could see and touch. He looked upon his preference as "the romantic way to go to sea." Long ago, someone had told him that if he was choosy he would not last in the business, and now he knew that he would take anything. He would ship out on a tanker, a freighter, a container ship, a bulk carrier (ore and grain), an L.N.G. (liquid natural gas), a Ro/Ro, or a LASH (its containers are hulls: they are lowered into the water and towed away).

On that first day in Charleston, there was nothing on the board. Elise Silvers, the dispatcher, told Andy that the Cygnus, a Lykes Brothers Ro/Ro leaving in a few days for Antwerp and Rotterdam, would be replacing its second mate. She could also tell him that a Sea-Land ship needing a third mate would be sailing in about ten days from Jacksonville to Bremerhaven. And roughly two weeks hence the S.S. Stella Lykes would leave Charleston for South America with a new second mate. Andy Chase found all this "incredible"—three openings in as many weeks—and, schooled to go for the earliest opportunity, focussed on the Cygnus.

The door opened, and Pete Pizzarelli came in—trim as a nail, beardless, dark-olive skin. He was, as Andy soon found out, a second mate. "I just got off the Allison," he said. "I'm sitting back and relaxing now. I'm night-mating. That's it." It was Andy's turn, for the moment, to sit back and relax as well. Which he chose not to do. Before the moment when your shipping card is exercised and actually takes precedence over all others, you never know what may come through the door and keep you off a ship. In Charleston, there was one daily job call—at one-thirty. At one-twenty-nine on the crucial day, someone could walk in with a truly killer card. And Andy could kiss the Cygnus goodbye.

With Pizzarelli, he talked ships—what else? Ships are all that people talk about in union halls, with the exception of politics as it relates to ships. This ship was built in Korea.

That ship was built in Germany. This one paid off in Houston. That one paid off in New Orleans. Where a ship pays off is where it most often changes crew members. Pizzarelli told a story from his last ocean voyage. Thousands of dollars' worth of ships' stores had been seized by pirates in Guayaquil.

That evening, while Andy and I were talking about something completely unrelated to the sea, he suddenly looked up and said, "It happens more often than you like to think. A nice fat job appears on the board. A guy strolls in off the street with a card that beats yours."

Peninsular Charleston is a small antiquarian Manhattan, lying between confluent rivers and pointing south into a substantial harbor. As in Manhattan, there is a battery at the southern tip, in the oldest part of the city. When you drive about the region, you are frequently looking over water. On the way to the hall the second day, I noticed a ship that had come in and anchored in Charleston Harbor—a freighter, indistinct in haze, at least three miles from the road.

I said, "Why don't we get on that one?"

Andy, who was driving, glanced to his left, and said, "It's a foreign ship."

"How do you know that?"

"It has writing on the side. Lykes and American President have writing on the side and it doesn't look like either of them. It's a stick ship and the house is aft. We have plenty of ships with the house aft, but not stick ships. We don't have many stick ships left, period."

Through the intervening water a long black shape was sliding, graceful as an alligator, and analogously fast. Andy noticed it first, out of the corner of his eye. He said it was a Trident-class submarine, five hundred and sixty feet long, and it could go at least fifty miles an hour; the exact figure was classified; the Navy would admit to twenty-three. Submarines can move rapidly because they are in a single fluid, he went on. There are no waves. Waves detain ordinary ships, which operate at the interface of two fluids. An idea that has been around for a long time is to make a very fast cargo ship consisting of two submarines with stems rising to a literal bridge connecting them, where the crew would be housed and the helmsman would stand. We weren't going to be shipping out on anything like that, either.

For the second consecutive day in the Masters, Mates, and Pilots hall, there was, as Andy expected, nothing on the board—no surprises, no new developments, no unexpected ships, not so much as one night-mating job, nothing to learn that he didn't know already. He was present for the job call, though—and in plenty of time. Andy never misses a job call. If he is in a city to look for a ship, he goes to the hall every day, regardless of what he may know. "You're counting on luck," he said. "A ship might come in a day early. A ship not on a schedule might come in." A ship not on a schedule is a tramp steamer.

The hall opens at nine. We learned that a mate named Tony Tedmore had been waiting there at nine to register for a new shipping card, and when the office opened a little late and he was handed a card that said "9:04" he had become furious and announced his intention to make a formal complaint to the union. Andy said, "When I paid off my ship last year, I hotfooted it to the union hall as fast as I could. Your former job ends. Your bargaining power begins. Every minute counts. At job calls, I've seen one person beat out another by as little as a minute on his shipping card."

After the obligatory vacation period, which has lately settled back to fifteen days for every thirty at sea, there comes the moment when you are permitted to look for work again, but there's scarcely any point in trying until your shore time grows longer. As people sit in union halls, the grapevine will tell them how old a card has to be to get a job. One long job begets another—the more sea time, the more vacation time, the older your card when you look again. You can get into a bind of short jobs. On the actual day when a ship you are hoping for is called, your card goes into a box on a table at the union hall. Anyone can look at it. This prevents "backdoor shipping." There was once a day when a couple of hundred dollars tucked under a dispatcher's fingers could get you a ship.

Andy has never refused a job because of something he has heard about a ship from gossip in a union hall:

"The captain's a tyrant."

"The captain's a creep."

"The captain's a drunk."

"It's a terrible run."

"The ship is unsafe."

"You never get any port time."

"They carry dangerous cargo."

Andy said, "You may find that the creepy old captain is a neat guy. Or he may be a recluse, but when all hell breaks loose he turns out to be a great seaman. That's why the company goes along with the guy."

Many dry-cargo mates fear tankers. When a dry-cargo ship ties up at a dock, longshoremen come aboard and unload her. When a tanker is in port, her own mates load and discharge the ship. The work is hazardous, and most dry-cargo mates don't know how to do it. "I still get trepidation when I go on a tanker," Andy said. "You're lining up a hundred valves. You're operating under the assumption that all valves leak. They usually do. We had oil in the pump room on the Spray. We calculated that to get there the oil had to go through six closed valves. It was an old ship. The fumes on a tanker are sometimes so thick you can see them rise like fountains. They spread in the air. They flow over the deck. You can see them go down the sides."

The door opened. In came a man with a sharp face, a sportive mustache, bowl-cut bangs the color of light straw. Andy had never seen him before. In this situation, two people who are unfamiliar will sniff each other out in seconds. This was Gene Whalen, second mate, out of Cape Canaveral, looking for a ship. He said, "I just go from port to port: Jacksonville, Port Everglades—small places." In the continuing conversation, he mentioned that he was a graduate of the New York Maritime College, at Throgs Neck, in the Bronx, that he enjoyed shipping with Lykes when he could, because "they're in a time warp, they're an easy-going company with break-bulk ships that stop in lots of ports." Dreamily, he spoke of Penang, of Borneo, of the mountain springs of Mindanao. He said that pirates had shot at his ship "in the Gulf of Thigh Land." He said, "Ping. Ping. You'd hear bullets hit the mast. You just duck." Piracy, one gathered, is heavy in the Strait of Malacca, in Guayaquil, on the whole West African coast. Pirates usually board ships in port. They come in boats to the seaward side of the ship. They throw a hook over the rail and shinny. They tie people up. They go for safes. In the Strait of Malacca, they attack moving ships. Crewmen line the rails with pressure-charged fire hoses to drive the pirates off the sides. Low-freeboard ships are especially vulnerable to pirates.

None of this interested Andy a ten-thousandth as much as the age of Whalen's card. Whalen eventually mentioned what it was. Andy had him beat to death.

The door opened, a new face came in—blond, heavy-set, linebacker man. Even a little cherubic. Curl across the forehead. Beard that could have been panned in a stream. Without a glance around, he walked right over to the desk to sign in for a job. He had just arrived in Charleston from his home, in Montana, and he didn't need to look for anything. This was, after all, the union of masters as well as mates. The paperwork he quickly completed is known as "clearing for a ship." Captain of the Sea-Land Performance, he would take over the ship when it arrived in Charleston. Captains and most chief mates are "permanent." They take enforced vacations like everybody else, but—at the owners' behest—they return to their specific ships. With rare exceptions, no second mates or third mates are permanent. Many unlicensed personnel have permanent jobs; most do not.

In the afternoon, we went to a couple of ship chandlers'. We talked with a fisherman about the fish he was not catching from the battery. We sat on a park bench under the deep shade of live oaks and squinted into the glare of the harbor. Andy said that he had begun to develop second thoughts about the Cygnus. He was unaccustomed to having any kind of choice. His experience instructed him to take the first open ship and risk nothing. Unfortunately, though, the desirability of the jobs before him seemed to rise from one to the next. He needed sea time. Second mates become chief mates not only by passing examinations but also by accumulating sea time. The Cygnus job was significantly short on sea time. For that matter, the Sea-Land trip out of Jacksonville was not what you would call an odyssey. Also, his daily wage and overtime pay would be lower with Sea-Land, because he'd be sailing as third mate. Jacksonville was something of a long shot in any case. And if he went down there he risked losing out on anything that might come up in Charleston in his absence.

The Stella Lykes was the most appealing ship. Second mate. Interesting run. All the sea time he wanted and needed. But to wait for the Stella Lykes meant weeks, not days, multiplying the possibility that something could go wrong. "It's a bit of a gamble," he said. "You never know if someone's going to come walking into the hall that day and take it away from you."

In less than a day, though, he made up his mind. He would break his own rules. He would pass up the Cygnus and Sea-Land. He would narrow the field and raise the risk. He would wait for the Stella Lykes. In the Merchant Marine, there is an expression that describes what he was doing. He was laying for a ship.

A couple of "Port Relief Officer Jobs" were posted on the board. Andy chose to night-mate the Sea-Land Performance from 1600 to 2400. On the same watch, Pizzarelli would night-mate the Cygnus. The two ships were ten miles apart. At midnight, Andy would drive the ten miles in nothing flat, and, further exercising the seniority of his shipping card, relieve Pizzarelli and work the Cygnus until eight in the morning. He would be paid twenty-three dollars an hour. He bought a pack of cigarettes. "If I have cigarettes and a cup of coffee, I'll feel so rancid I can't fall asleep," he said. At home in Maine, he almost never smokes. Night-mating, he has worked sixteen-hour nights back to back and gone to the union hall during the day. There, with his head on a table, he sleeps. Just before the job call, he lifts his head. Night-mating in Charleston, he would make a thousand dollars in less than a week.

A police officer with coconut palms on the lenses of

her eyeglasses admitted us to the Columbus Street Terminal, Old Charleston. We walked across acres of paved open storage under heavy-lift sheer-leg cranes. The dock was three-quarters of a mile long. The dimensions of the Sea-Land Performance were Panamax (fitting by inches in the locks of the Panama Canal). As we approached the gangway, Andy remarked that his "basic ambition" was "someday to be the skipper of a ship like this."

While he put in his eight hours making rounds—chronicling the opening and closing of hatches, noting degrees of inshore list, checking the ullage and innage of ballast—I did what I could to stow the vocabulary (if your gas tank is all ullage you are going nowhere), and I talked to the captain, Kenneth Ronald Crook. He was behind a desk in a spacious office, reachable by elevator, near the top of the house. Across the room, I sat on a couch by a coffee table. Like everyone else in the Merchant Marine, he told sea stories. One or two were a touch macabre. He said he had been on a Calmar ship that made regular runs to Los Angeles from Baltimore with steel. One of the ordinaries could not keep his hands out of the food. That is, time after time he walked the cafeteria line, reached across the cutting board, and sank a hand into a tub of food. Finally, the chief cook could not contain his rage. One day, as the hand moved over the cutting board, a cleaver came down and cut off the hand. The chief mate used a blowtorch to cauterize the stump.

On the same ship on a beautiful day with long low swells in the Pacific, a seaman was standing in the rigging on a ladder that was not tied down. As the roll of the ship reached its maximum angle, both the ladder and the sailor went over the side. A life ring was thrown to him. He got himself into it. A lifeboat was lowered. When the man was taken from the sea, only half of his body was there.

At least he was employed. Without a modulation of tone, Captain Crook went into the horrors of the search for work. "In those days—as third mate, second mate—I was shipping off the board. There were too many mates and not enough ships. I drove from York, Pennsylvania, where I lived then, to Baltimore every day, looking for a ship. There were job calls every two hours, so I was in the hall all day. Weeks would go by with no job called. Then a job would come along and I'd get beat out by someone else's card." After he got a ship or two with Moore-McCormack Lines and became a permanent chief mate, he discovered that working for shipping companies was not unlike working for magazines. Established structures (Moore-McCormack, the *Saturday Evening Post*, United States Lines, *Life*, Seatrain, *Look*) tended to collapse beneath you. After the Moore-McCormack ocean fleet was absorbed by United States Lines, in 1982, Crook "sat on the beach for seven months basically without a job." The union forced United States Lines to hire him. In 1986, United States Lines went bankrupt. "Thirty-some ships came to a screeching halt. That put an awful lot of people on the beach. A lot of the older skippers retired. Sea-Land purchased about twenty ships, including this one. I sat on the beach from the middle of February until November 17th. I was in the dentist chair in Montana. The union called from New York. I was to be captain of an old stick ship called S.S. Galveston Bay, taking food to the natives in Africa. Right down my alley. That job led to this one. From zero income to a six-figure income makes a difference." The difference was the ranch he had his eye on in Montana, with its hundreds of acres and its trout streams.

By midnight, Andy and I were on the bridge of the Cygnus, at Wando Terminal, on the Wando River. The air-conditioning on the ship had failed. The temperature was above a hundred. Through thick dust weighted with fumes, Army tanks rolled onto the ship. One end was open like the mouth of a sucker. The Cygnus inside resembled a tunnel. Taped to the satellite-navigation receiver on the bridge were recent advisories from the Maritime Administration on the subject of pirates. On the west coast of South America, the S.S. Mallory Lykes had been "boarded by one or more pirates with machetes." In the Strait of Malacca, the master of a South Korean vessel had been "beaten and forced to open the ship's safe by pirates who boarded the ship in the vicinity of Batam Island." Lying near the SatNav was a Maritime Administration brochure called "Piracy Countermeasures." It said, "Countermeasures should be designed to keep boarders off the ship. Repelling armed pirates already on deck can be dangerous. . . . Have water hoses under pressure with nozzles ready. . . . Use rat guards on all mooring lines and illuminate the lines. . . . Under way, keep good radar and visual lookout."

A ship in port can be filthy, hot, and dismal, in contrast

to the same ship at sea. Andy, staring forward from the bridge, seemed to be out there somewhere on the deep ocean, a very great distance from the Wando River. "You develop affection for your ship," he said quietly. "A rusty grimy disagreeable bucket soon becomes an object of affection." There on the Cygnus bridge—sweating marrow, reading about rat guards—I found it hard to imagine being affectionate toward the Cygnus, but not entirely impossible.

As time passed in Charleston, Andy got more night-mating work—Farrell Lines' American Resolute—but essentially he waited. At some point during the second week, his shipping card became eleven months old. "I'm up in the big leagues now," he said. "Basically, I think I'm all right, but it's healthy to be a little nervous." One day, he felt his health running over when a second mate arrived from New York specifically looking for the Stella Lykes. New York! Oh, Jesus! Andy thought. But he had the older card.

I was up at five-thirty on the day we expected the ship to be called. I read a long political article that included a catalogue of every national deficiency except the Merchant Marine. Andy slept until nine-thirty but got up nervous about the drawbridge. We left at ten-thirty to make the one-thirty call. Andy said, "This way, if we run out of gas or get a flat tire we can still make it."

I said, "We got gas last night."

We arrived in Charleston, of course, early enough to ship out on a Yankee clipper. We drove around. We exchanged worries. We killed ten minutes in a Burger King, and carried the food away, because we felt pressed. When we went into the union hall and sat down to eat and wait, Andy's hands were shaking. Lettuce fell out of his sandwich. He was unable to line up the straw that was meant to penetrate the lid of his takeout Pepsi. One o'clock. Thirty minutes to go. The door opened. Chester Dauksevich came in, the mate from New York with the inferior card. Beardless, tall, and going bald, with a white mustache, he wore brown leather wing-tip shoes, white-faded jeans, a guayabera. To destroy a few more minutes, I asked him why he had come to Charleston.

"Because I'm hungry and broke," he said. "There's forty guys ahead of me in New York. That's why I'm here. I might run out of money. It's costing me too much here."

Having been informed long since that this was to be the day of the all-important call, we had not been much concerned about the shipping board. One port-relief-officer job was up there, nothing more. At the job call, there was no mention of the S.S. Stella Lykes. The telephone rang at one-thirty-four. Andy's wife, MaLinda, standing in rain at a pay phone in Bucksport, Maine, wanted to know if he had a ship. No ship. He would have to wait it out for another twenty-four hours.

At that moment, the whereabouts of the Stella Lykes happened to be Port Newark. As Andy and I left the Charleston hall, I mentioned to him that Luke Midgett, the incumbent second mate, would be getting off in Charleston because his time was up, and, since he lived in Charleston and was well aware of the difficulties of getting a ship, could be expected not to go around telling the whole city of New York about his coming debarkation—but word could be got out of him. I confessed that, in my overanxious way, I had just thought of this and begun to fret.

Andy said, "That's why I was hoping the ship would be called today. Actually, all the people on these ships know now that you can get a ship out of Charleston. If they are talking, some people might hear that and come down here. Say there's almost no one in the union hall five days running, then a ship comes in and three guys show up from New York. They go on the company's ships there, which talk to other ships, and get advance word of who's getting off where. They could come tonight. They could come in the morning."

In the morning, he again allowed three hours. As we approached the Ben Sawyer Bridge, we saw that it was open. Andy turned off the engine, and we sat in the line of cars. Above the Spartina grass we could see the stack and the bridge of a slowly moving tug, bearing the insignia of the Corps of Engineers. Andy said, "Last year, down here in the Charleston hall, I saw a guy come in with an eleven-months-plus-thirty-days killer card and take a ship an hour before his card was to expire."

I said, "A lot of good that card would have done him if he'd been stuck behind this bridge."

The tug went off to our left, and the drawbridge swung closed.

"There's always anxiety about making the jump to a new ship," Andy continued as he drove on. "It has nothing to do with the competition. Suddenly it's time to go. I can sit in a hall for weeks and weeks just dying for a ship, and then when it's there I get all wound up. It's something like whitewater kayaking: you go down a long placid stretch of river, and when you hear the roar ahead you think, Do I really want to go through with this? It's always the same. It's true of practically everybody."

At eleven-forty-five, in the union hall, a sheet went up on the board:

**** OFFSHORE SHIPPING JOBS ****

COMPANY:	Lykes Bros.
SHIP:	SS Stella Lykes
LOCATED:	Wando
SAILS:	0300 Monday
RUN:	West Coast South America
JOB:	Second Officer
TIME:	120-day rotary
RELIEVING:	L. Midgett
REASON:	Time up

Visible through the glass door was a strange face, approaching. Was this the killer card? The man turned right and vanished into a men's room. The hall closed for lunch. In Applebee's restaurant, on Sam Rittenberg Boulevard, a sinewy, nautical, shaggy-blond, bearded man in a sleeveless shirt sat under an Uncle Sam poster ("I WANT YOU").

"He's looking for a ship."

"He came here in a new Mercedes."

"He's obviously a second mate."

At twelve-fifty-six, we were back at the hall, waiting for it to reopen. A man in an electric-blue shirt and dark glasses, obviously a merchant mariner, came up the stairs. It was John Abbate, second mate. We knew him already, and he was no threat. He owned rental units near Charleston, did a lot of night-mating, and was not looking for a ship.

At a quarter after one, there were footsteps on the stairs. Pete Pizzarelli appeared. Fifteen minutes to go and there were no killer cards from New York, or, for that matter, from anywhere else. Time to relax. Try telling that to Andy.

The door opened. Chester Dauksevich came in, wearing a Mets cap and smoking a Salem in a holder. The guayabera of the day was adorned with filigree.

Ten minutes to go and Andy's eyes were still flickering toward the door. Dauksevich, in response to a question, said that his high-school class was 1950 and he went to the Massachusetts Maritime Academy. Andy asked him how shipping was in the fifties.

Dauksevich said, "It sucked."

The telephone rang at one-thirty-one. MaLinda was calling from Maine. Yes, Andy had the ship: the Stella Lykes.

Dauksevich and Abbate signed on to night-mate her in Charleston. The various men present started to leave, telling Andy to say hello to this person or that on the Stella.

Dauksevich, surprisingly, said, "Where you going?"

"West coast of South America," Andy said.

Dauksevich said, "Don't get the clap."

There was a television set in the union hall, and it happened to be on for the two-o'clock local news. The Ben Sawyer Bridge was stuck open. It had been stuck open since twelve-forty, when its brakes had failed and it had swung too far.

Four A.M., 32.25 degrees south, sky overcast, an almost total darkness on the bridge. To all horizons, no light. We have seen one ship in six days, since Guayaquil.

This is the tenth of August, the antipodal mirror of the tenth of February. The ocean air is cool. The momentum of more than forty thousand tons is as absolute as the darkness. In no hurried way is it going to change. If a target should appear on one of the radars, Andy, in avoiding it, would try to preserve a cushion of at least two miles. Very slowly, toward six, shapes will form in the developing light. Anyone coming or going through the passageway to the wheelhouse passes through two doors. When either door opens, the passageway lights go out. The bridge has to be dark, so that more than radar can see into the night. Andy is pacing around somewhere, invisible. Vernon McLaughlin is at the helm. The autopilot has the ship, but Mac stands by the helm.

I have attached myself to the four-to-eight watch. It is Andy's watch. It is the watch of both dawn and sunset. Mac will tell you, "It's the *only* watch." Mac is an able-bodied seaman. Calvin King, who is also an A.B., is far up in the bow, on lookout. William Kennedy, an ordinary seaman, will relieve Calvin at five. That Kennedy's name is William is as little known to the crew as the fact that his wife's name is Ethel. The crew, like his neighbors in Savannah, call him Peewee. Andy, Peewee, Calvin, Mac: the second mate, the ordinary, the two A.B.s—the deck watch, four to eight.

Getting up at three-thirty every morning is not as difficult as one might think—not if, in the evening, you are asleep soon after eight. I wander around the ship all day, but I go to bed at eight. Suppose I were in Iceland—four time zones east—and were asleep by midnight and awake by seven-thirty. I would be setting and rising at the exact moments that I set and rise out here.

This is the twentieth day of the voyage. For this ship, a voyage is forty-two days and begins and ends in New York. Our present position is about as far south as the Cape of Good Hope. Almost all of Australia is farther north than we are. Halfway up a straight line between here and New York is a point in the mantle two thousand miles deep.

Mac's voice, in the dark, says, "This ship goes to coke country. This ship is hot as a potato."

The captain, who worries, can list dozens of disquietudes idiosyncratic to this run. Mac has just mentioned one. Steamship companies are responsible for what they carry even if they don't know it is there. Fines in six figures can make significant contributions to overhead. Stacked on the main deck and down in the hatches are five hundred boxes—the amphorae of this era, the containers that fit on highway trailers. The containers are sealed. Everywhere in the cargo manifests are the letters "STC" or the words "Said to Contain":

> Said to Contain 16,636 pounds of shower curtains, telephones, and wall clocks.
>
> Said to Contain 7,650 pounds of religious books.
>
> STC 6,000 kits for assembling black-and-white TV sets.
>
> STC panties de señora, five and a half tons.

Customs officials of six countries are interested in our ship. In Port Newark, they have turned out to greet her in very large numbers with dogs. Mac remarks that a white Cadillac with both front doors open was sitting on the pier once in Newark. When Mac went down the gangway and off the ship, someone inside the Cadillac asked him where he was going. "I said, 'Is that any of your God-damned business?' He said, 'Yes, it is.' He said he was the Man. He said, 'What have you got in there?' I said, 'Here, take it,' and threw it in the car. He said, 'Oh, it's your clothes.' I said, 'Whatever.' "

The first gray light will delineate the speaker at the helm—a man built strong and square-shouldered, with a large head, a regal paunch, an equitable mustache, and eyes that gleam with fun and anger. Not to mention moral indignation. Targets turn up on the radar. Fishing boats. Answering instructions from Andy, Mac turns off the autopilot and moves the wheel of the ship.

Andy is soon on the telephone: "Good morning, Captain, it's five-thirty. We are twenty miles out, and at our present rate of speed we should arrive at seven-ten." Normally—when we are at sea, and not about to intersect a continent—Andy calls the captain at half past six. No matter what the time is, the captain always answers quickly, and always sounds wide awake.

Gradually, the Fathometer has been sketching the steep slope of the Peru-Chile Trench, and the extremely narrow continental shelf. Electric lights come into view, rising high in sinuous lines, like ornamental strings in leafless trees. There are thousands of them, and they are beautiful. They define dark hills we cannot see.

We hear a door open and close. Another opens. Captain Washburn comes into the wheelhouse. "Good morning, good morning," he says. The first salutation may be for us, the second for the ship. More likely, the other way round. The captain routinely talks to the ship. Now, though, he goes directly to the radio. Channel 16. "Valparaiso pilots, Valparaiso pilots. This is the American steamship Stella Lykes. Stella Lykes. Whiskey, Mike, Romeo, Golf. Over." If you say those words—Whiskey, Mike, Romeo, Golf—in that order anywhere in the world, they mean this ship. In this part of the world, at the moment, no one seems to care. The captain waits in silence until his patience runs out. His patience could set a record at a hundred metres. Again he says, "Valparaiso pilots, Valparaiso pilots. This is the American steamship Stella Lykes. Stella Lykes. Whiskey, Mike, Romeo, Golf. Over."

No response.

"So much for moving ships at this hour in the morning," the captain says. "The port isn't even awake yet. When Ethan Allen was expiring, people said to him, 'Ethan, the angels expect you,' and Ethan said, 'God damn them. Let them wait.' Then he expired."

The complete resonance of the captain's parable passes above the head of the Person in Addition to Crew. In the dark, the captain paces back and forth across the wheelhouse. Andy is also a bridge pacer. Andy and the captain have long since developed a collision-avoidance system. "I don't stay in one place," the captain says. "I never did. I don't stay in one place even when I'm *in* one place. Give 'em a moving target."

The light rises. There stands Mac at the wheel, his eyes agleam. His visored cap is white. He is wearing a cardigan sweatshirt, bluejeans, street shoes—and the keys dangling at his hip are attached to a halyard clip. Andy is revealed on the bridge wing, out in the winter air, leaving lots of room for the captain. Andy is wearing a down vest, a light-blue shirt, jeans, and running shoes. Gold letters on his blue cap say "STATE OF MAINE." Andy has the metabolism of Eugene O'Neill. He is six feet tall and weightless. Food is squandered on him. He eats ravenously, gains nothing. His stomach is flatter than a deck. His hair is reddish-brown and halfway covers his ears. His beard is rufous, too. His eyeglasses, lacking rims, invest him with a professorial veneer.

Across the front of the wheelhouse are ten large windows, rounded at the corners, providing an interrupted view of the sea and the enlarging city. The lashed containers are visible now, stacked so high that they block the line of sight from bridge to bow. On top of some of the stacks, riding far up in the sky, are bulldozers and earthmovers and big backhoes that look like thunder lizards. There is a small fire engine, white with red trim.

Andy telephones Peewee, who is on lookout in the bow. Now that dawn has passed, Peewee can knock off. As Andy puts down the phone, he says reflectively, and with some feeling, "There's no sunrise in the engine room."

In front of the bridge telegraph and the redundant radars and the redundant steering mechanisms lies a long rubber mat, which firms the footsteps of anyone traversing the bridge. With the captain present, it is not a good place to linger. Back and forth through the wheelhouse he moves, from one bridge-wing door to the other—now indoors, now outdoors and a spin around a binnacle, now indoors, now outdoors and a look over the side. Occasionally, he stops and talks to someone. Sometimes he just stops and talks. Out of the blue, I have heard him say, "A little here, a little there." Out of the blue, I have heard him say, "If you don't like to do that, seek gainful employment elsewhere. The army of the unemployed has an opening." Out of nowhere, I have heard him say, "O.K., ye of little faith, there has been a change in the program; the regular cast has left and the stand-ins are taking over." With no related dialogue coming before or after, I have heard him say, "Any jackass can do that." Quite evidently speaking to the ship, he will sometimes say, "I don't like to lose and I never quit." Often he asks questions and then provides answers. One day, offering advice to all within earshot, he said, "In Rome, do as the Romanians do." His political opinions are unambiguous. Adlai Stevenson was "a wimpy little coward mumbling platitudes." The President of the Republic of Panama is "a pineapple-faced bum." The United States has been reduced to "a choice between being poor-and-weak and poor-and-strong." Pleasantly, he says, "You can get all the vitriol out of me you want, because I'm loaded with it."

This captain runs a happy ship. There are personnel aboard, both licensed and unlicensed, who have patterned their time and risked unemployment in order to sail with him. He has not won them over with fraternization. In the same unvarying manner in which Pinckney B. Ezekiel is called Zeke and Trevor Procter is called Kiwi and William Kennedy is called Peewee, Paul McHenry Washburn is called Captain Washburn. His family's early background is deep New England. His middle name relates to the fort of the star-spangled banner. He knows what a magisterial distance is, and he knows how to keep it.

"He's wrung more seawater out of his boots than I'll ever sail across," Andy says of the captain, awarding him the status of a marine cliché.

When Luke Midgett, the old second mate, was getting

off the ship and turning his job over to Andy, he remarked of Washburn, "He's a wonderful old man. He doesn't bother you. He likes for you to do your job and do it thorough. He's a big thing on these national flags. Make sure the flags are up. If you don't, the country will write a letter." Jerome Pope, one of the A.B.s who sought their jobs because Washburn is the skipper, has told me that Washburn is "a good captain, a senior captain, a good ship handler with a lot of experience, who doesn't hassle the crew and isn't all scared to death of that Lykes Brothers." In the radio shack, William Raymond Charteris Beach, who is known in this milieu as Sparks, will tell you that Washburn is "confident of the sea." Beach goes on to say, "He knows his job. He is strict. He will bring the book down, but he runs a happy ship. I have sailed on ships with a captain who is sarcastic with the chief mate to the point that the mate won't talk with him, and if the ship was going to run aground he wouldn't tell him." Washburn will talk to anybody. If he sometimes seems to prefer talking with himself, there's an obvious reason: he's the most interesting person on the ship.

Now about to dock in a foreign city, he is wearing his more-or-less-dress blues. His shoes and trousers are dark and naval. His white short-sleeved shirt, open at the collar, has epaulets striped with gold. There is gold braid on his visor. His glasses are rimmed with gold. As he moves back and forth on the bridge, he takes things in with the comprehensive gaze of a boxer. He leans forward like a boxer, his mouth and jaw set firm. His body is chunky, his paunch under control, like a trimmed spinnaker. Wisps of gray edge his cap. His face—beardless, full-featured—appears to have been the site of an epic battle, wherein the vitriol he speaks of has at last been subdued by humor.

The day's first light displays the breakwater, the harbor, the hills of Valparaiso. The coastal plain, if one can call it that, runs a few blocks to the rising ground. The community sweeps upward many hundreds of vertical feet on hills that descend into deep sea. The harbor is just an artifact stuck to the hull of the continent. When big swells come in, as they often do, on a long reach across the Pacific, they can shake out the basin and render it absurd. "The swell comes right over the breakwater," the captain remarks. "I've seen green seas on top of the docks, water running uptown. Ships break free and go off the pier." Years ago, as an able-bodied seaman, he came down here on a stick ship called Gulf Merchant. It broke twenty-three lines tied to the dock at Valparaiso.

Today, the breakwater is effective; the harbor ahead is evidently calm. The pilot boat at last approaches. "Mr. Chase, please run up the Chilean flag," Captain Washburn says. "We won't offend their delicate sensitivities, their national pride and honor." After a pause, he adds, "Chile is the best-run country in South America. And *we* would like to change it."

The words of the harbor pilot are, technically, advice. When the captain repeats them, they become commands. Half ahead, slow ahead, dead slow ahead, steady as she goes, slow astern, the ship maneuvers toward the dock. On the engine-order telegraph, Andy relays the commands to the engine room, where the telegraph rings a bell. This is known as "giving them bells." When J. Peter Fritz gives them bells, he sometimes calls first on the telephone to say, "Did I wake you? This is the chief mate."

Eight stories below the bridge, in the basement of the house, Graham Ramsay is on the maneuvering platform. In response to the bells, he shouts: "Ahead slow!" "Half astern!" "Stop!" His hands move from wheel to wheel—from throttle to throttle to guardian valve. The commands he relays send David Carter and Phillip Begin running into the fireroom to twist knobs above burners, altering by hand the flow of fuel and air. Begin, whose name is pronounced like "Keegan," is the chief engineer. He is not required to twist knobs, but he is everywhere that matters when things are going on, and functions in a style that ignores his rank. He has a quick smile, blue eyes, hair that falls beyond his ears, a youthful handsome beardless face; and he has eaten very well. Carter is the demac on the four-to-eight watch—deck and engine mechanic. He used to teach Spanish in Florida public schools and now, from books in his cabin, he is teaching himself engineering. He runs into the fireroom, comes back, wipes his forehead, and shouts, with striking emphasis on certain words, "Up on the *bridge*, they think they can speed up and slow down with *ease*. They don't realize we're scurrying around like *rats* trying to do what they *want*."

Up there eight stories, as they do their gavotte among Chilean warships, they approach the berth against the backdrop of the seaport, the steep and populated hills. Down here, there is no Valparaiso. There is no sense of place. What attracts the eye is flashing colored lights. We could have made a landfall on Long Island. We could be nosing into the Gowanus Canal. "Stop" or no "Stop," "Slow astern" or "Half ahead," there is no sense of motion, either. Instead—among the burners, the boilers, the turbines, the tubes—there is noise. The company supplies the earplugs. If you don't use them, a day will come when you cannot hear your alarm clock.

Graham Ramsay is the first. This stands for first assistant. He is known as the first because he is the second-ranking engineer. Near him stands Karl Knudsen, who is known as the second, because he is the third-ranking engineer. Knudsen is young, trim, aviator-handsome, with a competent mustache. He came up the hawsepipe, by way of a union school in Baltimore. He wears white leather shoes and green coveralls, and says, "In my business, appearances don't count." Ramsay is a tall man with an experienced face, a friendly and vulnerable look, gray hair—United States Merchant Marine Academy, 1956. Because he is standing on a platform, his head is about seven feet above the deck, in a warm place. The engine room is full of hot spots. Its storied heat is by no means uniform. In the Panama Canal the temperature at Ramsay's head was a hundred and twenty-eight degrees, but of course it is milder in this midwinter Chilean sea. It is not quite a hundred and ten. There are places in the engine room that generally exceed a hundred and fifty degrees. People don't stand around in them much, but sometimes they have to—for example, if they are painting. Phil Begin, shouting, points out that the ship's cold-water pipes unaccountably cluster in the engine room, and that is why the house is full of hot toilets. I have a thermometer with me. When I put it in my pocket, my leg cools it off. A step down from the maneuvering platform is the engineers' flat, where a logbook lies open on a standing desk and the engine watch can loiter under four large blowers. In the course of a sea watch, the blowers and the water fountain provide the only relief available in four hours. The blowers are a foot in diameter and, somewhere above, are sucking in outside air. It picks up heat on its way down but feels good as it pours out. People stand under the blowers in much the way that people stand under showers. On some ships, they stand in the airstream according to rank, with the chief engineer farthest upcurrent. David Carter shouts in my ear, "Some guys just stand under the blower and don't do jack shit!" The blowers are always the coolest spots in the engine room. In the Caribbean, the temperature under the blowers will typically exceed a hundred and ten degrees. Some people, over time, grow to like the engine-room heat—like it to the point of need. There is a sailor aboard who plugs up the air-conditioning vents in the ceiling of his cabin in order to get the temperature up to a hundred and ten degrees. Here in the winter South Pacific, the temperature directly under the blowers is eighty, and the temperature in the rest of the engineers' flat is ninety-seven. These are the lowest temperatures that the engineers will experience during the entire voyage. Like a bottle in a bucket of water, the engine room is immersed in the sea. Sea temperature is to the engine room what air temperature is to the bridge. The sea temperature at Valparaiso is fifty-five degrees. The Caribbean reaches ninety.

"Stop!" Ramsay shouts, and Carter and Begin run through the fireroom to the burners. The fireroom is not an enclosure but a space framed by two boilers, each fired by three burners. Above the burners are red and green and yellow lights. The yellows are flashing. The emergency override is deliberately ignoring the sensor's electric eye. Elsewhere, the red lights of the flame scanners are steadily blinking. "Slow ahead!" Ramsay shouts, and, a minute later, "Stop!" Begin and Carter adjust the burners. They may be stopping while a mooring line goes out, but the engineers don't need to know. However, they are human, they are curious. In the Panama Canal, they did not even know if they were in the locks. In Gatun, the chief went up for a look. He came down and reported, "We're in the locks. There's a Maersk ship ahead of us. The rope handlers are coming on." Under the blowers, faces looked up with interest.

"Slow astern!"

The burners, on either side, are numbered one, two, three. When Begin and Carter run to them, they are like football guards pulling out to execute a play, and they have to remember similar signals. Only the twos and threes are involved in a "Stop," the ones and twos in "Half astern," two and two in "Slow astern," "Dead slow," "Slow ahead," and "Half ahead"—if head winds and currents don't force one of several alternative patterns. Feed water is all-important. It must be present or there's a meltdown. There's a big red box in the fireroom. It contains, by law, nine cubic feet of sand.

"Stop!" Ramsay shouts again as he spins a wheel. When Ramsay pays off in Charleston, he rides Amtrak home to Delaware. A man who can spend four months in an engine room at sea does not require an airplane to whisk him home. On his way north in the train, he sits by the window to watch the country. Across the eleven hours, he undergoes a land change. When he pulls into Wilmington, he is ready to be there. "FINISH WITH ENGINES!" he shouts. Ramsay, Begin, Carter, and Knudsen take the steam off the turbines, break the vacuum on the main condenser, and extinguish four of the six burners. One does not need a periscope to infer that the ship is tied up in Valparaiso.

Few of the watches that begin at 4 A.M. turn up the lights of cities. Most watches have a rhythmic sameness, plunging through the dark, with the scent of coffee percolating on the bridge, the scent of bacon from five decks below, Mac or Calvin invisible at the wheel, Andy the Navigator—every inch an officer in his bluejeans, running shoes, rolled-up sleeves—working with dividers in the chartroom under a dim red lamp. In the first nine days on the Pacific, we put into port only once. One morning, a couple of hundred miles off the Colombian coast—at five-forty-nine, the hour of dawn—we heard in the wind a distinct whinny.

We saw whales on the way south, and were led by porpoises. Albatrosses flew beside us, motionless to the point of impudence, their eyes on our necks, their great wings fixed, their iron momentum matching the ship's. At bridge level, sixty-five feet above the water, an albatross flew beside us with his right leg up scratching his ear. But not even that was as weird as this whinny, in ocean air, so far from land. We knew, of course, where it came from—and the whinnies that followed as well—but knowledge didn't make the sound less strange. Andy said, "These are not the horse latitudes."

On Hatch 4, Bay 1, about halfway between the bridge and the bow, were four containers said to contain twenty-four thoroughbreds. One of them was Dr. Sab, out of White Reason by Seattle Slew. Undefeated in five starts, Dr. Sab was on his way to race in Guayaquil. So was The Admiral. So was Axe Lady. Most of the other horses were nameless two-year-olds on their way from Royal Eagle Farm, in Panama, to the stables of Silvio DeVoto, in Ecuador. To tote nine tons of horses eight hundred miles, Lykes Brothers was charging six thousand eight hundred dollars. For a few hundred more, the company was providing the food and lodging of Carlos Rolando Lopez, who described himself to me as the "assistant trainer of the principal horse, Dr. Sab." Carlos numbered among his intimate friends the Panamanian jockeys. Jacinto Vasquez. Lafitt Pincay, Jr. Walter Guerra. Jorge Velasquez. Carlos said that his own mentor was Luis Ferrugia the Magician, "the best trainer in Panama City." Carlos made these remarks, among other places, over meals—where, from a Xeroxed menu, I helped him choose what he wanted.

Carlos was eating better than his horses. I went to Hatch 4 with him in the afternoon. The containers were stowed amidships with their doors open. As many as seven horses were in one twenty-foot box—in narrow wooden stalls framed within the steel. The two-year-olds were cribbing as if their lives depended on it. They were chewing up the wood of the stalls. Five hundred miles from Guayaquil, they had already made crescent-shaped indentations larger than slices of watermelon. They were chewing the posts as well as the rails. Carlos explained that they were hungry. He said a very strict diet of hay and water was the Magician's formula for avoiding seasickness. Unfortunately, someone had taken the great trainer too much at his word and had sent to the ship just eight little packets of hay. Carlos was not being democratic. He had been giving a full ration to Dr. Sab, somewhat less to Axe Lady and The Admiral, and pittances to the others. Two and a half packets of hay were left. Carlos was reserving it all for Dr. Sab. This son of Seattle Slew—and brother of Slew City Slew—was a black horse that looked unpleasant, but the wood of his stall was whole.

I left Carlos and went to the bridge. The captain was attentive to the horses and asked how they were getting along. Vernon McLaughlin was at the ship's wheel, and as the story unfolded he burst out, "They're so fucking cheap they won't feed their horses. With wood in their stomachs, they can't pass it. That's a sin!"

"Carlos says that is not a problem," I told him. "Carlos says, 'They could eat the whole ship.' "

Mac would not stoop to comment.

Time passed. A further thought occurred to me. "Dr.

Sab is undefeated," I remarked. "Impressive as that may be, he has run in only five races, and he is five years old. What has he been doing?"

Captain Washburn said, "He's been eating."

Those were watches of targets and rain. The weather was so heavy one morning that when the light came up we couldn't see the bow. Peewee was on lookout in the bow. Calvin King was at the wheel, standing somewhat heavily, tired—Calvin, from Weldon, North Carolina, a grandfather, in his tortoiseshell bifocals, his Lykes Brothers cap, his khaki shirt, his brown leather shoes, his bluejeans patched in the seat with cloth of another color. Andy was leaning over the north-up radar, marking the plotting head with a grease pencil. Calvin said, "This ain't no workin' weather. I'm too old for this shit." He was referring not to quartermastering—his turn at the wheel on the four-to-eight watch—but to overtime work on the open deck, which would fill his day between eight and four. Two of the windows in front of him had spinning circles of glass set like bifocals into the panes. They whirl so fast you can see through rain. But not very far that morning.

Targets had been appearing on the radar in close abundance since the watch began. At four-thirty, in clearer air before the rain, two ships were ahead of us—six and a half miles and nine miles distant. The nearer one was lit up like a city and might have been anything from a passenger vessel to a fish processor. On the farther ship, a green (starboard) light was visible. Was she crossing to the right or was she not moving? On the plotting head Andy marked their positions with the grease pencil. The plotting head is a Plexiglas screen that fits above the radar screen and is illuminated from the sides in a way that emboldens the wax from the pencil. Calvin, to whom these collision-avoidance procedures amounted to nothing more than background routine, was saying that when he goes off the ship in Panama he does not like to stray much farther than the duty-free shop at the end of the pier. "If there's fighting, you might catch a .38 or a .44."

Andy kept his nose on the radar and made two more marks with the pencil. In time, he responded to Calvin, saying, "I don't like those low temperatures."

Calvin, who has described himself as "an old country boy," likes guns and collects them. He has been looking for a nine-shooter .22 revolver for his wife, but a nine-shooter .22 is not easy to find. He may have to settle for a .32. "A .32-calibre pistol with a three- or four-inch barrel on it is a woman's special," he has told me. "It's not as big as a .38, and a woman can handle it."

The radar's nearer target was four miles away, and Andy still made no course change. He was convinced that the ships were not moving. The nearer one had red over white over red on her mast, signifying that she was restricted in her ability to maneuver. She could be a seismic ship with a two-mile cable. Andy picked up the short-range transceiver. "Calling one of two stationary vessels approximately thirty minutes north, eighty degrees west," he said. "This is the southbound ship a few miles north of you." There was no answer. When the targeted ships were three and a half and four and a half miles away, Andy told Calvin to take Stella off the iron mike—the autopilot—and "put it on hand" (Calvin's hand). With a three-mile cushion, we passed two large stationary fishing vessels—one improperly lighted. Minutes later, four new targets appeared on the radar, about ten miles away. Andy made two course changes that moved the bow twenty degrees, and he pressed a button called Trial Maneuver on the Automatic Radar Plotting Aid of the Collision Avoidance System, which showed him what would happen at any course and speed he might choose. In the terminology of this machine, "CPA" meant "Closest Point of Approach." In the event of a flat-out plate-buckling tectonic crash, the machine would let you know that you had "Zero CPA." The spread of four ships was now four miles away. With a final glance at the machine, Andy chose a heading of a hundred and seventy. He said to Calvin, "Left to one-seven-zero."

Calvin said, "Left to one-seven-zero. One-seven-zero, hand steering."

We went past the targets and, for the moment, into the clear. From the bridge wings we could see the lights of seven fishing boats and three merchant ships. The merchant ships were following us. We had overtaken them. To look far down over the side at light from our ship on the racing dark water was to feel the power of the weighted glide, its controlled uncontrollability. We were a bowling ball, avoiding duckpins.

Andy changed the heading back to two-one-zero. As we headed into a line squall, a radar target on our left seemed to insist on crossing our bow. Andy said, "She's coming down my hawsepipe. Fishing boats maneuver so much you don't move on them until you're close enough to know they won't turn." Then he swung right and passed the target, a mile and a half away. The rainstorm, on the radar, looked like a sweet potato.

Andy enjoys his work with the radar, and, by his own matter-of-fact description, is good at it. He can look at the screen, see multiple targets, and sense the geometries of course and speed. He intuitively grasps the direction of ships even before he has plotted their paths with dots and streaks. He has a sense of deceptive landmarks. He can look at a radared coastline and not be fooled by cliffs that appear to rise from the water but in fact stand far behind a beach. He has spent a good deal of time in the radar-simulator laboratory at the Maine Maritime Academy, where there are four named practice rooms: Andrea Doria, Yellowstone, Ponce de León, Stockholm. What the Stockholm was to the Andrea Doria the Yellowstone was to the Ponce de León. "Radar work is my strong point," he once told me. "I feel that I can outmaneuver a lot of people with the radar. Overtaking a boat is more dangerous than it seems. She's out there for a long time, and a steering-gear failure, or whatever, has more time in which to occur. It's like slowly passing a tractor trailer. You think about the jackknife."

A seagoing lieutenant in the United States Navy once asked me if merchant ships have radar. After learning that they do, he asked if the mates use grease pencils. He seemed surprised. Merchant mariners, for their part, tend to characterize Navy people as green and earnest. They joke about the redundant multitudes that inhabit a Navy-ship bridge. There is a story much told by Navy people and yachtsmen about a merchant ship steaming somewhere at nineteen knots with a dog on the bridge, alone on watch. Andy and I call a tale like that an asmut: an apocryphal story much told. One such yarn, which he told that morning, led up to a question that was supposedly put to a merchant skipper as he arrived in port: "Captain, have you seen any sailboats recently?"

"No."

"Well, you should have. There's a mast and rigging hanging from your anchor."

Without taking his eyes off the north-up radar, Andy said, "Yachtsmen like to tell that story. Merchant seamen see yachtsmen as bozos, but I've been with yachtsmen who could teach some seamanship to merchant seamen. Yachtsmen see merchant seamen as people who cruise with no one on the bridge. Yachtsmen display poor seamanship, too. There are more cases of yachts creating problems for big ships than big ships creating problems for yachts. We need a mile of cushion around us, at least. There are a lot of yachtsmen who are out there just to drink beer."

The difference between the ten-centimetre radar and the three-centimetre radar has to do with detail versus range, and has nothing to do with north up. Either radar can be set that way—with north at the top of the screen, as on an ordinary map. I have been referring to the ten-centimetre radar as the north-up radar because that, at the time, was how the world was presented on its screen. The ship was steaming south, so targets ahead of us, as they showed up at the bottom of the screen, appeared to be behind us. In this sense, the plotting of targets was backward. When the north-up feature was added to radars, it caused no little annoyance. "You can do more with north up," Andy said. "Modern sailors are trained that way; the old-timers were not." The north-up advantage in maneuvering is that watch officers do not have to replot the position and the course of every target on the screen each time they change course themselves. On north-up radar, you are moving through the real world, and not through an artificial seascape determined by the vector of your ship. Andy, facing the bow and leaning over the screen, had no difficulty understanding that the Stella Lykes—as represented by the screen's center—was moving not toward the bow but toward him. This was too much for Captain Washburn. In the way that a person driving south with a road map will turn it upside down the better to comprehend what lies ahead, Captain Washburn wanted his radar screen aimed in the direction of the ship. Of the three-centimetre radar he said that morning, as he did virtually every morning, "Leave it on head up for me." When Andy joined the ship and Washburn told him how he liked things done, Andy asked the captain if he wanted the radars north up or head up. Washburn said he knew that more could be done with north up, "but always leave one of them on head up for me."

From the privacy of his cabin, on the boat deck just below the bridge, Captain Washburn can look forward past containers and over the starboard sea. He tends to linger over the view when he is uncomfortable about an officer on the bridge. As he describes it, "I stand a lot of watches from my window."

Asked if he sleeps well on the ship, he says, "I have made trips where I couldn't sleep at all. The main thing is to have people who will call you when trouble is imminent. I say to the mates, 'I'm not supposed to sleep. Courts don't think so. Call me early, don't just call me up here to be a witness.'"

I have asked him how long it takes him to become comfortable with a new chief mate, second, or third.

"Sometimes almost right away," he said. "Sometimes half a trip. Sometimes I'm never totally sure but I'll just kind of take a chance. I pick the watches that I can sleep on. I can sleep on any of these."

In certain concatenating circumstances, he has remained awake for as many as seventy-two consecutive hours. "I made trips to Vietnam where, on the coast, I stayed awake as long as I could, got the ship into shallow water, and anchored it, and lay down and slept for a few hours, and got up and picked the anchor up and went on, because I was not going to sleep on the coast with *one* of the men that I had. In the middle of the ocean, I'd have hoped they wouldn't run into somebody. But if there was land or rocks or coastwise things or small boats or fishermen to run into . . . they weren't doing it. On one ship, the only man I could rely on was the chief engineer. That included the radio officer, the other licensed officers, and all of the unlicensed crew. This was at the height of Vietnam. When you talk to the veteran seamen, they'll all tell you that was the worst—I mean, personnelwise. Over the years, there has been a slow change in the personnel in the Merchant Marine. We don't have the knife fights, the broken-bottle fights. They're isolated instances today. The people are older. They are more steady. Hey, there are more people who are dependent on this job to support a family."

Which did not necessarily mean that he would trust them on the bridge. "In crossing and passing situations, you have a privileged vessel and a burdened vessel," he said to the four-to-eight watch, and the dialogue that followed had some subtle bifurcations. While ostensibly educating me, he included messages to Andy. While not exactly lecturing to Andy, he reassured the ship. "I wouldn't have a person around that wanted to hold on to a crossing or passing situation in which a chance of collision was prevalent," he continued. "The old rule was that the privileged vessel held its course, the burdened vessel had to give way. They followed that rule for a hundred years and piled up one ship after another. The privileged vessel was required to maintain course and speed until such time that only action by both vessels would prevent collision. You had to hang on so long that even if only you took action it was too late. I myself never hung on to a situation that long, even though that was the court interpretation of the rules, and I didn't abide my officers' hanging on to it that long. We were out of there before the situation got that close. The rule has been changed now. You are not required to do that. You have more leeway to play with. It's more a question of prudence and good seamanship now. When I see certain ships, I seem to have some kind of an instinct that says, 'Hey, give this guy a little more room.' In ship channels and rivers, you pass fifty feet apart all the time, but that don't mean it's apropos to do it in the middle of an ocean. Hey, it's just like driving, out here. You sail defensively. You cannot depend on that other fella to always stop at the stop sign or not change lanes or give you the right of way or use his blinker signal. You can't count on him to do anything. Hey, the *only* way I'm going to get hit is in the stern. Somebody faster who is really after me is going to have to run me down and hit me in the stern."

In the *Merchant Marine Officers' Handbook*, I found a reprinted article called "Tips on Practical Shiphandling" by Captain H. A. V. von Pflugk. One of those mornings on the way to Guayaquil, I carried the book to the captain's cabin and read this passage to him:

> If . . . you feel, when laying your hand upon the rail, that you are in contact with something alive, responsive to your slightest touch, something that is a part of you, something that you really love, then you are in a good position to become truly expert at shiphandling—if you have the knack and are gifted with good judgment and have an eye for distance and are the calm rather than the excitable type.

He said, "You're singing my song. I don't fancy myself as those things, but the love that I have for this business . . . I've spoken to you about being emotionally involved with ships. I get carried away by it sometimes—ships that I really liked and ones that I didn't care for. But the opening part of that . . . To feel that I am part of a living thing and that I love what I'm doing and would rather do this than anything else . . . I'd rather be here than anywhere. Whether I am gifted with those other things I would leave for someone else to say. I might fancy myself that I am. But when I put my hand on a rail and think that I am associated with a living thing, and that I cannot only control it but that I have something going with it, we understand each other. It isn't all me taking and her giving. We work as a unit. I talk things over with her, and almost ask her, 'Hey, can we do this?' I am not just demanding what this ship can do for me, I'm asking what I can do for her. 'Look, old girl, you're in trouble. Let's see if we can help each other.' "

There had been a recent moment when the old girl was in trouble. In Cartagena, we drew a pilot of whom Washburn said, "He can't dock a ship. He can take you from the sea buoy to an anchorage. He can undock you and take you out. But he goes all to pieces when he gets close to a dock coming in. There are a scattered few of us around who can't play golf. He can't dock a ship."

The pilot lived up to this job description. Dead slow, the six-hundred-and-sixty-five-foot Stella Lykes—as large as most old-time ocean liners—entered its designated slip, which it would share with the Colombian freighter Ciudad de Manizales. Stella would tie up on her portside. A firm wind was blowing across her port quarter. The mistakes made by the pilot were several. He misjudged the wind. He had a tug pushing Stella on the wrong side. To put the bow in, he called for full ahead when he was very close to the dock.

The stern swung wide of the bollards it was trying for, and toward the City of Manizales. The water narrowed between the ships. A collision seemed imminent. There is one place in the world where pilots are in absolute charge of ships, and the place is not Cartagena. (Pilots are supreme in the Panama Canal.) There is always some insurance risk if a local pilot is ignored, and plenty of insurance risk if a local pilot is not aboard. Washburn has said, "Your worst enemy can be your own underwriter. If I'm in Borneo and a guy comes on board with a spear in his hand and a bone in his nose and says he's the pilot, he's hired." Now, however, this man in Cartagena had come on board with a pencil in his hand and a bone in his head, and misjudged the wind and misused a tug and called for full ahead within inches of the pier. Washburn literally stood him in a corner and took the ship away from him. The Colombian freighter was twenty feet away. In a tone that contained no panic, Washburn said to Andy, "Get a stern line to the pier with a small boat if you can." Meanwhile, he maneuvered: sculling, in effect, to preserve his distance—engineers running among the burners as Washburn gave them bells.

Ships are tied up with what the rest of the world would

call ropes. They look anachronistic—like rope you would see in a seaport museum, but larger. A good mooring line costs eight thousand dollars. Made of Dacron for strength and polypropylene for flexibility, it is six hundred feet long. We carry eighteen. As a mooring line payed out over the side and reached like a suspension cable in the direction of the pier, the ship was so askew that the six hundred feet might not do. You marry one line to another if the need arises. In Genoa once, on the Almeria Lykes, Washburn married three lines and winched the ship more than a thousand feet. The one line spanned the distance here and was soon secured to the bollards. A dugout canoe passed below it, moving smartly under a sail made of flour sacks. Very slowly against the wind—completing what Washburn would later call "one of the poorest dockings in marine history"—Stella reeled herself in.

Captain Washburn's family name derives from Great Washburne, near Evesham, in the English Midlands. The McHenrys in his background of course were Scots. John Washburn of Evesham immigrated to the Massachusetts Bay Colony in 1631. The family were in coastal shipping in the Boston area before going into timber and allied enterprises in Maine. In lake-and-river country near New Hampshire, they had a hilltop farm called Norlands—hundreds of acres and long deep views—that might as well have been called a plantation. It looks today much as it did a century ago. As Norlands Living History Center, it attracts school buses and preserves its first demeanor. There is a widow's walk on top of the house, for a widow with exceptional eyes, Norlands being fifty miles from the sea. Samuel Washburn (1824-90) was a skipper of clipper ships, a captain in the United States Merchant Marine. Elihu Washburn (1816-87) was named Secretary of State and minister to France by Ulysses S. Grant, whose portrait is prominent in the freestanding Washburn Memorial Library (1883), with its spinning wheels, its Britannica IX, its rose and pale-blue windows. Washburns went west, founded the Minneapolis Mill Company, and made Gold Medal Flour. They were involved in the beginnings of General Mills. Washburn College, in Topeka, Kansas, is named for Ichabod Washburn. The father of our Captain Washburn was a Washington lawyer. ("He had the trait of honesty. Hey, he didn't have a chance.") As a schoolboy in the District of Columbia, aged thirteen, Paul McHenry Washburn was told to write an essay about an ancestor. He wrote about Chief Justice John Marshall. He turned in the essay, but he was not for school. He ran away from home.

The captain learned from Leadline Dunn, from Terrible Terry Harmon, from Dirty Shirt George Price. These are the old skippers with whom he sailed when he was young, and on whose seamanship he modelled his own. They were not his only icons. He had plenty of admiration for Herbert P. High Pressure Erwin, for Clean Shirt George Price, and for Rebel Frazier. He even learned from Wacky Wacker. He had less affection for Jake the Snake Jacobs, Tanktop Evans, and Wild Buck Newsome. With the exception of Tanktop, who was an engineer, all were skippers. Some were still mates when Washburn sailed with them.

He sailed on Liberty ships. He sailed with the International Freighting Corporation, the Luckenbach Steamship Company, the United Fruit Company, the Mystic Steamship Company, the South Atlantic Mail Line. He sailed with Lykes Brothers Steamship Company. Dirty Shirt George Price and Clean Shirt George Price were not related. Each man, as it happened, was named George F. Price, Jr. Harmon was Terrible Terry when he was a first mate. Later, he renamed himself Harmless Harmon. Washburn says, "He was called Terrible Terry because of his personality. He was his own worst enemy. But he knew the sea. He knew ships." Leadline (whose nickname rhymed with "deadline") was actually John Dunn. Among these first-class seamen, Dirty Shirt and Terrible Terry were especially gifted in the art of stowage and also had high reputations for "protecting ships and protecting people." Their example became Washburn's fixed priorities, which he lists as

1—people
2—ship
3—cargo.

When he himself became a master, and a difficult situation came up, he would think of the old skippers. He would think, If they threw this at Dirty Shirt, what would he do?

Dirty Shirt was a short man with "inky-black hair and cold dark direct eyes," as Washburn describes him. "Two hours after he shaved he looked like he needed a shave; he was of small stature but commanding, no less a man than a man six-four." Leadline had legs like beer kegs. "Rebel Frazier was a husky six-footer, dark visaged—he scowled. The closest thing to a smile was just not a scowl. He laughed once a month. He was not hostile, but there was no friendship in him. He was an excellent ship's master. He knew the sea. He knew ships. He knew cargo. He knew weather. He had that instinct for dead reckoning that the old-timers had to have, because if you didn't have it you didn't make it." Dirty Shirt, Rebel, and Leadline instilled in Washburn the importance of confidence in your own dead reckoning: "Never doubt it. Never—as in do not ever—doubt it. Leadline came up in the twenties, when you didn't have a lot of navigation things to help you. You did it on your own or you fell by the wayside." Washburn went on to say, "The old skippers did all their own piloting, docking, and undocking. They were their own agents. They did all the ship's business. They'd go up to the customhouse to enter a ship and clear a ship. They did the manifests. Each was a one-man floating industry. Leadline had a sixth sense as to what types of wave action and sky action hint at coming weather. I learned to read the sky from him. From him I learned things not to do. Leadline was an aggressor in dealing with people. A steamship master—while he's there—*is* the master. Leadline and Dirty Shirt and Terrible Terry—they did not back off from anyone. I learned from them to maintain a gulf between yourself and the other officers. I learned, Never cross that gulf. I learned, Don't act like the other officers, dress like them, or socialize with them. I learned, Don't be like them. Whatever they are, be different. Never waver in your dealings with them. Don't vacillate. I learned, Never chastise people in public, even if they have earned it. I learned, Don't alibi, don't complain."

Tell it to the ship.

Now sixty-five years old, the captain began as an ordinary seaman in a Merchant Marine of fewer than a thousand ships and saw it rise above two thousand ships and then decline by eighty per cent. He has seen at least fifteen American shipping companies go ventral in the water. Only three major ones remain alive in international shipping: American President Lines, Sea-Land, and Lykes Brothers Steamship Company. Ship for ship, crew lists have become much shorter as well—a process known as reduced manning, which is the result of a combination of automational technology and economic constraint. Ships that might once have had fifty in the crew now have twenty-one. Some ships are so undermanned that extra people have to come out from land to help dock them.

From No. 1 in the world in total ships, the United States Merchant Marine has dropped to No. 13, while Panama and Russia are ascendant, with Liberia not far behind. In the world competition for cargo, American-flag companies sail under heavy overheads of taxes, insurance rates, and crew costs, while ships under other flags are much less encumbered, and the Russian Merchant Marine, which often underbids everybody, is a hobby of the state. The wages of American crews are at least four times as high as the wages of crews sailing under many foreign flags. Federal construction subsidies have long since been removed. These are not the economics of a winning bid, and the fleet continues to shrink.

The situation long ago gave rise to open-flag registry —to the so-called flag of convenience, the convenience being that taxes could be avoided, insurance could be to a considerable extent ignored, and wages attractive to shipowners could be paid to merchant sailors drawn from any part of the world, if ships were registered in countries that would permit and fashion such a package. If you were a flagmaker, at this point you would have wanted to get out your Panamanian rectangles. As small nations catered to the balance sheets of alien shipowners, their services became known as boutique registries. Evergreen, flying the white star of Taiwan, has been described as "the leading foreign-flag company in the world," with crews of only sixteen or eighteen and "monthly salaries roughly equivalent to the weekly pay of American sailors." You can register a ship in the Republic of Vanuatu. A ship wholly owned in Kansas City can sail under the flag of the Sultan of Oman.

Carnival Cruise Lines, of Miami, Florida, consists of three ships under the Liberian flag, one under the Bahamian flag, four under the Panamanian flag, and three under the Dutch flag. Great American Lines, recently bankrupt, was a hundred per cent Liberian. Great American Lines had one ship. The Connecticut Bank & Trust Company owns two ships, both Liberian. Exxon has sixty-two ships, under ten flags, including eight under the Argentine gold sun, five under the French tricolor, and twenty flying the Union Jack, which has become a flag of convenience as Britain sells the waves. The Amoco fleet is entirely Liberian. The Chevron fleet is twenty per cent American, nine per cent British, fifteen per cent Bahamian, and fifty-six per cent Liberian. Texaco has thirteen ships, none flying the American flag. Mobil has thirty-six ships under seven flags, including the flag of South Africa.

Three hundred and forty-one ships owned by Americans sail under foreign flags. Some of the owners patriotically refer to these ships as the Effective U.S.-Controlled Fleet, a term regarded as a risible euphemism by, among other people, the maritime unions and Captain Washburn. In his words, "a ship owned in Chicago, with a Burmese crew and Spanish officers, will not go where you want it to in an emergency."

The crew of Stella mutters:

"Lykes Brothers could go foreign-flag like the rest of them, and sail with Balearic Islanders."

"You can hire people to chip paint and fill an oilcan, but who's going to rebuild a Westinghouse turbogenerator?"

"We can't compete with countries that pay sailors one dollar a day and feed them fish heads and rice."

The United States has not been the only loser in the international competition. As cargo rates have fallen below levels at which companies can operate profitably, a revolution has occurred in the merchant marines of the once preeminent maritime nations. They have been forced to "flag it out." Norway has accomplished this by creating its own foreign flag—the so-called Norwegian International Flag—and giving up the tradition of the all-Norwegian crew in favor of alien sailors. As a Norwegian-ship manager has explained to me, "maybe the master, the chief engineer, and the chief mate are retained, and paid ten to fifteen per cent less than before, but the rest are gone, they are running laundromats, they have been replaced by Far Eastern officers and crew, the pay and fringes were too much." Sweden, whose shipyards once ranked second in the world, has ceased to build oceangoing ships. All through Scandinavia, safety-training schools are empty.

Because flag-of-convenience ships are essentially unregulated, they have led a trend toward compromised safety and the lowest practicable levels of operation and maintenance. Dragging others down with them, they have crowded into a genre previously reserved for Greeks and Haitians. As viewed from the wheelhouses of the American Merchant Marine, the butts of jokes—the oafs of the oceans—have long been the Greeks and the Haitians: unseaworthy-sailors-let-loose-in-unseaworthy-ships sort of thing, the worst on water, ship handlers of such negligible skill that one ought to cede them wider clearance than anyone else in the world with the exception of the United States Coast Guard. So go the stories. If there was any distinction, the Haitians had the worst vessels, the Greeks the worst sailors. In Vernon McLaughlin's words, "Greeks are known throughout the world as very bad seamen." Captain Washburn recently watched the Haitian vessel In God We Trust going out of Miami in a condition not likely to attract much confidence from any other Source. "Haitian ships have no electricity, no electronic instruments," he says. "No fish, no food. They load beyond capacity, and off they sail. More than two hundred ships a year are lost out here, all flags. They're unseaworthy, they're improperly loaded, they have leaking hatches, metal fatigue. In God We Trust was never heard from again."

He continues, "A lot of us who have put our lives into this thing don't want to see the Merchant Marine die. It is not only worthwhile but necessary. Every hundred million the government has pulled out of Merchant Marine subsidies has probably cost billions in mounting trade deficits. We pay other flags, including Russia, millions of dollars to deliver our foreign aid: rice, flour, vegetable oil, powdered milk, tanks, jeeps. By law, fifty per cent is supposed to go on American ships, but we don't have the bottoms. Some years, we carry five per cent. Even so, our shipping companies are more dependent on our foreign aid than the foreigners we aid. We have not only one of the smallest but also one of the most aged merchant marines. Most of our ships are *beyond* their normal life expectancy. American shipyards have been folding, and their skills with them. The shipyards that remain are essentially repair yards—Bath, Newport News, Chester, Pascagoula. That's it. That's all she wrote, hoss."

While the United States Merchant Marine and the merchant marines of all the traditional maritime nations have struggled to compete with boutique flags and remain economically under way, the expanding competitiveness of the Soviet Union has not eased anyone's burden. The Soviet Union long ago decided that one good way to be much involved in the world's activities is to carry the goods. Ninety-five per cent of the world's freight travels on the sea. Annually, the Russian Merchant Marine carries fifty times as much cargo as the United States Merchant Marine. The Soviet Union has been spending about two and a half billion dollars a year on shipping development. It has bought many trade routes, and it is building so many ships that it may soon be ordering them from Western yards. It is so eager for business that it has planned to test an ice-strengthened freighter that could cross the Arctic Ocean hauling lead and zinc from Alaska to smelters in West Germany—all to save one week, shortcutting the alternative route, through the Panama Canal. "Russia is going to have five thousand merchant ships in ten years," Washburn says. "And we are going to have none—enn, oh, enn, ee, as in not any."

He remembers when F-14 fighter engines travelled to Israel in Russian ships, it being cheaper that way. The Russians give good weight. Not only were the F-14 engines "defense sensitive"—that is to say, classified—they were by law supposed to go in American bottoms. But what American bottoms? The Russians, on a routine basis, run a couple of hundred ships in and out of American ports—more than half as many ships as there are in the entire United States Merchant Marine. A story that Washburn savors less than some others involves the importation of chrome, and its crucial importance to United States industries. The chrome came from the part of Rhodesia that is now Zimbabwe. When, for moral reasons, the United States government imposed economic sanctions against Rhodesia, American business executives made of moral coral were obliged to figure out how to circumvent the sanctions. It was not a great problem. For a three-hundred-per-cent premium, Russians showed up with the chrome.

In the warm flows of amity that now connect the two nations, Washburn is an ice cube. "The ocean is one more country to take over," he says. "They may have had trouble taking over Afghanistan, but they're having no trouble taking over this ocean. They go to an international conference on freight rates and sign an accord agreeing to a rate of, say, eighty-two dollars a ton; then, immediately, they offer space for thirty-seven dollars, or whatever. Same song, second verse."

He also says that a typical Russian merchant ship has at least two naval-trained officers, a K.G.B. man, and a commissar who runs the ship, telling the captain what to do.

Not long ago, a sailboat on Lake Michigan capsized in a storm and the crew spent seven hours clinging to the hull. They were rescued by a Russian merchant ship.

If Dirty Shirt George Price had a shipful of starving horses, what would Dirty Shirt do? If they threw this at Dirty Shirt, what would he do? Captain Washburn found an answer. He sent word to the galley that he wanted all the corn, cereal, bread, and other foodstuffs that the cook could possibly spare. Toward noon, when the cook had got it all together, the captain asked me to find Carlos and bring him to the bridge. I went to Hatch 4, Bay 1, where Carlos was offering the horses generous amounts of water, and accompanied him to the bridge. The captain, with obvious pleasure, asked me to tell Carlos that he had set aside for the horses a hundred and twenty ears of corn.

Understand, I am by no means fluent. I have a fairly good Spanish vocabulary, an ear that seems to reject incoming Spanish sound, and grammar tartare. The pleasure in my voice must have been clear enough, though, as I told Carlos about the corn.

Carlos said that racehorses do not eat corn—not *his* racehorses, anyway. Absolutely, they were not to be given corn.

While the helmsman listened and the chief mate listened, I repeated this to Captain Washburn.

The captain's demeanor changed. In brusque staccato, he said, "Tell him to be my guest, then, if the horses prefer wood." Becoming even more sarcastic, he continued, "Tell him I'm sorry I don't have barley or oats."

I said that the captain had no other grains.

Carlos said that the captain needn't worry. The horses were not to be given other grains.

I told Carlos that the captain was sorry.

Carlos said, in English, "No problem." In Spanish he said to tell the captain that everything would be all right if we arrived on schedule in the morning. Was the captain quite certain that we would arrive in the morning?

Washburn said, "Tell him I can't say whether we will arrive at seven-fifty-five or eight."

Carlos remarked that by morning he would have one packet of hay left, which he would reserve for Dr. Sab.

To the captain I said, "Carlos feels confident that he can make it on one bale of hay and two cords of wood."

The captain said, "To each his own. Tell him I will no longer attempt to project myself into his business. Tell him I'm going to throw the corn over the side. Tell him I once had a rhinoceros on board."

Carlos said, "The captain has much experience."

Carlos went back to Hatch 4. When I saw him there

a short time later, his hands were purple with gentian, and he was nursing a wound. In the wind, pieces of his trousers flapped like flags. Inside a container, he had been climbing from one stall to another when a two-year-old bit him in the crotch.

Sometimes I go on lookout with Peewee, Mac, or Calvin—go forward with a flashlight on the main deck at four, up the ladder to the fo'c'sle deck, around the windlasses and the anchor chains, and past the hawsepipes to the absolute point of the bow, where the lookout station conforms to the requirements of admiralty court, being "as far forward and as low down as conditions allow." The lookout stands in a roofless cupboard. A sheet of clear plastic deflects the wind. He is not quite like a fly on a bowsprit, but somewhere near it—projected far over the water, over the nose bulb, and riding up and down the Pacific swells. He stands there, and stays there, in rain and lightning. He is transferred to a bridge wing if the weather gets rough and he lets the mate know that "she's taking green seas." In Peewee's words, "When we're taking sprays over the bow, taking seas up here, we go to the wing. It don't happen too much on this run. This run mostly calm all the time." The lookout reports the ships he sees, describing what has long since appeared on the radar. He reports wooden boats that the radar doesn't see. He looks for debris, floating objects, life rafts. We occasionally pass through a fishing fleet as if it were a cloud of gnats. Peewee says, "I report the first one and leave the rest to the mate. They all start turning on lights. There's too many to report. They fish in the dark.

Sometimes you're right up on them before they turn on their lights." Mac remembers when the lookout rang a bell if he saw something to starboard, rang it twice if to port, and three times if an object was dead ahead. He even remembers when lookouts shouted, "Lights are bright, sir!" and the mate on the bridge shouted back, "Aye, aye!" On this ship, it would have to be some shout. The distance from bow to bridge is four hundred feet.

The A.B.s stand the first hour—Mac on odd-numbered days. Then Peewee the ordinary takes over and remains through dawn. One odd-numbered night with no stars, Mac said he could not care less about the clouds of the Pacific and their harmless rains—he was just happy that this was not a run to North Europe. He said, "That run is never good. It is foggy in the summer; rough, cold, damp, and miserable in the winter." Sometimes in the winter North Atlantic, lookouts are posted around the clock.

At ten minutes to five, Peewee came on, and he also told lookout stories about the North Atlantic, which were summed up in one remark: "You can't see nothing. You just listen." Here, in the breaking dawns, he sees whales and porpoises and schools of tuna. Peewee was a housepainter before he went to sea. In Savannah, he has seven children and a number of grandchildren. He has been shipping out for thirty-five years. I asked him why.

"You make a good living. I just come and make my little time and go back." His sea time last year was six months. He made thirty thousand dollars. In Savannah, if the pay is acceptable, he will still occasionally paint. Not long ago, he painted a parachute tower at the Army airfield. He made seven hundred dollars a week—only a little more than half of what he earns at sea. Working high in the parachute tower reminded him of painting the masts of ships. For the most part in Savannah, he enjoys himself and works at nothing. He drives his Lincoln, and he pesters Ethel Kennedy. Soon he will retire.

"Will you miss being out here?"

"Oh, no. I'll miss the money, but that's it. If I want to see ships, I'll go to the waterfront. But I don't want to see them."

Our ports of call do not interest him. In fact, they frighten him. "In Valpo, they cut the third mate's pocket right out to get his money," he told me. "If you go to the bank to change money, they be watching you. In Valpo, when I finish at eight o'clock at night I just go to bed."

"What do you think about while you're up here on lookout?"

"I think about what I'd be doing if I wasn't here. I'd be partying. It's Sunday morning. I'd just be getting home by now. I don't drink anymore. I eat too many eggs. I had to stop drinking when I got the 'lesterol."

Peewee said he remembered being on lookout in the North Atlantic when there were "icebergs all around." He said, "They looked like diamonds in the night." He was in waters off Greenland on a tanker that carried jet fuel and discharged it at anchor after divers went into the water and brought up the ends of pipelines. As the ship approached the anchorage through fields of icebergs, there were lookouts with binoculars on both bridge wings. An icebreaker led the way. The ship hit no ice going in, but while she was at anchor ice hit the ship. Twenty-seven plates cracked.

The light came up—a gray Pacific dawn. Peewee materialized: a slight figure in a construction worker's leather boots, paint-spattered dungarees, a khaki wool shirt, and a baseball cap numbered 117—his daughter Louvenia's unit in the Air Force. Toward six-thirty, he said, "Should be time for sunset?"

"Sunset?"

"Yes. At sunset, that's when the mate calls you to knock off the lookout. Four-to-eight watch. I see the sun go down. I see the sun rise." Minutes went by, the gray became brighter, and still Andy did not call. At 06:41:36, the telephone rang in the bow. Andy said to Peewee, "Good morning. This is the equator."

Andy drops money on the equator. I wondered how much he was dropping on it now. I imagined myself throwing money on the equator, and shivered at the thought.

I also shivered in the cool of the morning. At noon that day, one degree south, the Fahrenheit temperature was seventy-eight degrees, the relative humidity seventy-five per cent. At noon that day in New York City, I learned later, the temperature was eighty-five and climbing. The day's high humidity was ninety-one per cent. All through the summer, everybody in New York and its perisphere had been living in the sort of climate that seals the skin and pops veins in the head: They waded in humidity. Every day for weeks, the high temperatures remained between eighty-eight and ninety-seven. Before I shipped out, I met a Liberian who had come to Princeton on a fellowship. I asked him if he liked America. He said, "Everything but the heat. It is intolerable. Never in my country have I experienced such heat." By comparison with New York, Panama was cool. The canal, creeping through the forest, was cool. The evening we left Panama, the temperature in the North Pacific was in the seventies. The weather was almost unnerving. As soon as Stella crossed the equator, you heard people say, "It's winter now"—a technicality that is not persuasive there at the latitude of Borneo, with the hull's velvet slide over that soft ocean. We entered the Gulf of Guayaquil. Just the sound of that name—Guayaquil—spelled coffee and chocolate to me, spelled mangoes, bananas, guavas, and heat. At four that afternoon, though, when the temperature in New York City was eighty-nine, the temperature in the Gulf of Guayaquil was seventy-five. I finally understood where the tropics are, why the nights of the iguana are on Forty-seventh Street, and Broadway steams with rain.

The captain said, "Bring her over smartly—zero-seven-five."

Calvin, at the wheel, said, "Zero-seven-five."

The mouth of the River Guayas is defended by a bedrock ledge, which at mean low water lies a few inches deeper than the keel of the Stella Lykes. Gingerly as she goes, every judgment must be perfect above the bar. ("We've been aground twice here," said the bosun.) The emerging current sweeps across the bar. There are large, powerful eddies.

"You slow down in here, she really goes sideways, she really goes like a crab," the captain said. "I watched her set down on this buoy here just to see how far she'd go. Zero-seven-three."

Calvin: "Zero-seven-three."

Andy said, "I see an impressive current on the buoy." The turbulence downcurrent from the buoy resembled the wake of a ship.

Our speed was reduced to ten knots. Burgos the river pilot, who had come aboard, wanted dead slow. Not on this ship in these waters, the captain said. "On dead slow, she doesn't steer. They made the ship a hundred and fifteen feet longer and they didn't change the rudder. You have to play high water here to come over this bar."

He played high water. Like a slaloming kayak, he came over the bar. The Fathometer, lacking the sophistication of a slide calliper, showed no discernible gap between the bottom of the hull and the top of the rock.

Captain Washburn said, "So far so mundane."

A wrecked stick ship lay before us in the mouth of the river—its hull canted, half submerged, its booms at gruesome angles in the air. "See that ship dead ahead?" Washburn said. "He shouldn't have gone there, on account of he's there forever."

As we entered the continent—to run forty miles upriver in the drainage due west of the Amazon—the temperature at 7 P.M. was seventy degrees. The sailors were wearing jackets and sweaters. It was the most refreshing air I had felt in two months—in a country named for the equator.

"The river current on the ebb tide, she comes out of there pretty good," Washburn said. "It's hell if you sheer off a thing and hell if you suck into it." As the propeller pulls water from under a ship, the ship goes down a little in the stern. "Going over the bar, we were down by the stern by fourteen inches. Here in the river, she is also smelling the bottom. She'll suck toward whatever you want to stay away from—a hump or the bank. A ship sucks into a bank or sheers off a bank. One way or the other, *something* is going to happen. Depending on the depth of the water, the horsepower, the tide, the currents, the unconformity of the bottom, she'll suck in or sheer off if she builds up a wave of water. On this river, if you're the man at the wheel you can't be learning on the job. You have to sense that sucker's going to move and put that corrected wheel on then, before it moves, or you're zigzagging all over the place and every time you chase that sheer around you're making it worse. There's some guys that have been steering all their lives and have no instinct for it and can't do it anyway. In a place like this, a good quartermaster is worth his weight in gold."

Calvin grew a foot at the wheel.

I said, "Suppose you had a neophyte where Calvin is."

Washburn said, "He panics. You go aground, you run into a buoy, or you hit another vessel."

Calvin—with authority burgeoning in his low, slow voice—remarked that he never had cared for electrical steering. He said, "You don't feel your ship."

We went up the river in darkness through a braid of

mangrove islands. At the maritime port of Guayaquil, in the glare of quayside light, pirates hit the ship while it was docking. The event was swift, incredible, prophetic, and surreal. It was also rehearsed. It could not have come off as smoothly had it not been rehearsed.

In the general profusion of sea stories, there had been so much talk about pirates that I was certain we would never see them. All through a voyage while nothing happens, sailors tell stories about things that happen. There is usually some connection with an ocean voyage, but sometimes the tales drift to the beach and into the streets and back rooms and beds. Apocryphal stories are much told: many a sailor has enough first-person sea stories to fill up several lifetimes. Andy has said, "If you added up a lot of people's sea stories, these people would be two hundred years old." After enduring such a monologue, one sailor will interrupt another to ask, "Did you sail bosun with Columbus?" As Stella went up the Guayas, a sailor said that we were arriving early "to give the pirates more time to take stuff off the ship." There were tales full of grappling hooks, bolt cutters, and crowbars. That nothing was going to happen seemed fairly clear until a fast boat with a quiet engine came up on the offshore side—slipped between the two tugs that were working the ship—and seven or eight pirates threw grappling hooks and swarmed across the rail. They climbed to a container, broke the seal with bolt cutters, removed half a dozen cartons said to contain the worldly possessions of an American diplomat, and were gone in five minutes. The captain appeared with a pistol stuck in his belt that was four times as large as a .45. It was a hand cannon. Its bore could have accommodated a golf ball. It glistened with Rhodesian chrome. It was a Kilgore P52 flare gun loaded with a twenty-thousand-candlepower parachute flare. I had seen the box of flares: "Danger—Extremely Flammable, Keep Out of Reach of Children. Directions: Fire Upward." The captain said something about "getting one of them bastards," but surely he meant to follow the directions. Besides, it was too late. The boarders were gone. "See?" he said. "You come on a modern ship and you are attacked by pirates—by a little outboard flying the Jolly Roger."

On the fifth of August and again far out to sea, Calvin had the first turn at the wheel. I asked him what day of the week it was. He had no idea. Like everybody else, he knew that it was the fifteenth day of the present voyage, but the day's heathen name meant next to nothing. On Sundays, by some metaphysical process that is not well understood, most of the crew appear in fresh clothes. Calvin's khaki shirt has an iron shine. On Saturdays, the second mate goes up and down the house winding the ship's clocks. Essentially, though, the days are homogeneous. Calvin and I, adding on our fingers in the dark, needed several minutes to figure out that it was Friday. What truly mattered to most of the crew was how many days there were to go: twenty-nine if you were paying off in Charleston after the end of this voyage, seventy-one if you were making the next trip, too. Here by free will, and (in most cases) with histories behind them of decades on the sea, these people act like prisoners making Xs on a wall. I was to hear Jim Gossett say to William Kennedy one morning, "Peewee, we're under fifty days now. Forty-nine to go." This brought to mind graffiti I had seen on the State of Maine, the training ship of the Maine Maritime Academy. As part of the curriculum, students spend two summers on the State of Maine. The graffiti said, "ONLY 13 MORE MFD'S, ONLY 12 MORE MFD'S, ONLY 11 MORE MFD'S," and so on down a toilet stall. The "D" stood for "day." To me it seemed a strange thing for someone to write who was going to college to go to sea. But no professional mariner would fail to understand it.

This was one of the clear nights when Mars, Jupiter, and Venus were lined up like ships, steaming past Aldebaran on the way to Sirius. To port was a quarter-moon, and somewhere off the curve of the earth was Punta Pariñas, the westernmost cape of South America. We had entered the waters of Peru.

When you do that, you let them know. Peru wants to be notified at once that you have entered its waters, and to be told your position at eight in the morning and eight in the evening as long as you remain. For each failure to comply, the fine is five thousand dollars. William Raymond Charteris Beach—i.e., Sparks—would let them know.

Dawn came. The air, Fahrenheit, was sixty-two. There was a head wind at Force 7. The sea was heaping up, and there were whitecaps everywhere, and high spray, and the foam off breaking waves made streaks in the direction of the wind. At five-fifty-five, Vernon McLaughlin arrived on the bridge to relieve Calvin. Mac had spent the first hour of the watch standing in the bow in the fifty-mile compound wind, and the second hour swilling coffee. Now, taking over as quartermaster, he said, in his Cayman baritone, "Good morning. Happy birthday to me, too."

With no prodding, McLaughlin continued, "Fifty-eight years old today. I'm getting as old as Ronald Reegin."

I reached for a crew list and said to him, "You and everybody else, Mac. Calvin is sixty-one. Peewee is sixty-two. Sparks is fifty-nine. Jim Gossett is fifty-seven. Steve Kruthaupt is sixty-four. Bernie Tibbotts is sixty. Paul Agic is sixty. Frank Patton is sixty-one. Zeke is fifty-eight. Murray the ordinary is fifty-nine. Kiwi is fifty-three. Victor Belmosa is fifty-two. Louis Smothers is sixty. Duke Labaczewski is sixty." I had been pondering the crew list for days. There were thirty-four names on it. They included Robert Bryant, a thirty-year-old demac; Ron Peterson, the twenty-eight-year-old third mate; Karl Knudsen, the twenty-nine-year-old second engineer; and Donald Colon, the twenty-four-year-old engine cadet (a student from the United States Merchant Marine Academy at Kings Point, New York), not to mention Mr. Chase, the second mate, aged thirty-two. Yet the average age of the crew was fifty-one. "This is now an old man's business," the captain had remarked one day. "Sailing A.B.—it's an elderly gentleman's job." He didn't say anything about sailing captain.

As it happens, our six A.B.s average fifty-five years of age—ten years younger than Washburn. The captain is accustomed to sailing with crews averaging five to seven years older than our crew. He said he looked upon this as "a young ship."

McLaughlin continued to bestow upon himself his birthday honors. "Thirty-nine years at sea," he said. "All I need is feathers and I'll get up and fly. I'll be a seagull." Like everyone else in the crew—like Victor Belmosa, who was born in Trinidad; like Bill Beach, who was born in Scotland; like Trevor Procter and Bernie Tibbotts, who were born in New Zealand—Mac is an American citizen. He was born on Cayman Brac. The Cayman Islands were British colonial then, and Mac is a self-impelled transfer from the U.K. merchant fleet. The first vessel he worked on was a sailing ship. His father was her third mate. They picked up lumber in Alabama and took it to the Bahamas. When Mac hears the expression "iron men in wooden ships," he does not develop nostalgia. Moving up to steel, he worked on banana boats, making runs to London from the West Indies, Central America, Ecuador, and Colombia.

"I knew everything about bananas except how they talk. If they get below fifty-four degrees, they're dead. You might as well have taken a shotgun and killed them."

Some days, he comes into the wheelhouse in the dark of the early morning with bananas he has bought ashore. He buys forty-eight pounds, green as limes, for a dollar. Other people buy bananas, too. While theirs remain green, Mac's assume the color sunbeam. There may be, say, five hundred bananas on the ship all bought at the same time from the same dockside vender, and Mac's by a long interval will always be the first to turn yellow.

"I put the gezoong on them and they just turn ripe."

The gezoong is an amazing molecule in which two atoms of hydrogen are combined with one of oxygen. In his cabin each day, Mac wets his hands and flicks water from his fingers onto the bananas. He closes the box. When they are ready, he will come up to the bridge with a bunch in hand and say, for example, "These are Gros Michels. They are virtually square in cross-section. They have more squares than Locatans or Robustas. You will like them best. They don't appear to choke you."

McLaughlin is not only the four-to-eight-watch bananologist. He is the four-to-eight-watch ornithologist. When a man-of-war bird perched in the rigging, Mac said, "He knows better than to get his ass in the water—he won't get back out. He can't swim. He's not web-footed." While albatrosses were soaring beside the bridge, Mac said, "They can only take off into the wind and land into the wind. The only time they land is when they mate. The albatross is the soul of a lost seaman." When the man-of-war bird came back, Mac said, "He could pluck a pin out of the water. He chases other birds, beats the shit out of them, and takes their food."

Mac may be fifty-eight, but his eyesight seems to be 29-29. He will say, for example, "Pilot whales to port," and minutes go by before other people see them. He is the first to see oncoming ships. From the bridge of a tanker off the coast of Algeria he once spotted a floating mine, a lethal relic of the Second World War. The tanker's captain said, "He saved the ship," and served him Kool-Aid at the wheel. Mac will see islands fifteen miles away while others see nothing but blank horizon. Possibly he owes this ability not so much to his exceptional vision as to his birthright in the sea.

I asked, "How many degrees north of the equator are the Cayman Islands?"

He said, right back, "Eighteen degrees forty-five minutes. See how quick I answered that?"

He described the Grand Cayman of his youth as "a sleepy little island with dirt roads," and went on to say, "Now it has high-rise condos, superhighways, and five thousand banks." Cayman Brac, his home island, was eighty miles from Grand Cayman and was perched on the edge of Bartlett's Deep, the deepest part of the Caribbean—something close to twenty-five thousand feet. Bartlett's Deep is known in geology as the Cayman Trench, where the Caribbean crust dived under the North American Plate, melting far below to rise as magma and form volcanic islands. It has since become a different kind of fault, in history similar to the San Andreas. I said as much to Mac. As he looked at me, the always varying gleam in his eyes seemed for the moment to be ten per cent tolerance and ninety per cent pity. He said, in so many words, that if I thought I was talking about the Cayman Islands I was talking bullshit. He said he would henceforth call me Elisha. The biggest liar in the known history of Cayman Brac was Elisha. He was a fisherman who trolled for kingfish, wahoo, and sailfish, using a small herring as bait. One time, he got a fish on his line that pulled him around the eastern part of the island for four hours. When Elisha finally managed to boat this mighty fish, it was smaller than the herring. According to Elisha.

When McLaughlin was a teenager, he went out in a catboat fishing with a cousin "in the Grouper Hole, off the eastern end of Cayman Brac, eighteen fathom deep." Groupers spawn there in January. Mac and the cousin used hand lines, with small herring on the lines, and big sinkers. They caught so many huge groupers—each thirty to forty pounds—that they filled the catboat too full to sail. They paddled for Cayman Brac. A wind arose, and waves came over the cockpit coaming. The catboat sank. The boys swam ashore. The air sacs in the groupers expanded, and three thousand pounds of fish floated to the beach, where a grateful population gathered them up. According to McLaughlin.

He said, finishing the story, "In those days, I was the number-one fisherman."

McLaughlin's father went on shipping out until he was seventy-four. Mac will, too, if there's a Merchant Marine that will have him. "When I go ashore after this trip, I'll be fluttering like a fish out of water," he said. "I'll want to get back. It's an evil you want to come back to."

Mac lives as a bachelor in an apartment in Brooklyn. He has one son, who is in the Royal Marines, and they are out of touch.

I asked Mac if he had another job ashore.

"I'm a seabird," he answered. "When I'm at home on the beach, I don't work for nobody. All I do is lift a fork. I may have as much as six months when I get off here. It'll take six months before I'll have an old enough card to get a job. Years ago, you could get on a ship, put your clothes in a drawer, and throw your suitcase over the side. The ship was your home." Years ago, he sailed with a man who had been on one ship, with no vacation, for sixteen years. ("Brazil–New York, the romance run. He probably had two households.") Mac shipped out with Moore-McCormack until the line folded. Then he shipped out with United States Lines—on the American Michigan, the American Draco, the American Lynx, the American Legacy. The legacy was that the Lines folded.

This summer, he had gone to Savannah looking for a ship. "There's hardly any jobs going into New York anymore," he explained. "They don't pay off there. There's no ships being called there. When I left New York, I had close to a killer card. I had to get a ship in Savannah or forget it. If I didn't get a ship in ten days, my card would have died." In Savannah, his card got him onto the Stella Lykes over fifteen other able-bodied seamen.

"I remember when the union was strong," he said. "The union has gone from a big blow to a breath of wind." He told a sea story to illustrate the power of the National Maritime Union. The American Legacy was in Los Angeles when her television failed. The crew refused to leave port. Their contract called for a working nineteen-inch color TV.

While the ship remained at its berth and the wharfage fee mounted and another ship waited for the berth, the port agent went off shopping for a nineteen-inch TV. For some reason, he couldn't find one. Finally, he returned with a twenty-four-inch TV. When it was working, the American Legacy sailed.

"To the Far East," Mac said. "That was a long ocean voyage."

Now there were fewer ships and a scarcity of jobs; the union was weak, and its members were unemployed.

"Their stomachs are breaking like seas on a reef. And how many merchant ships are under construction?"

Andy answered, "None, in American yards."

Mac said, "That's a God-damned sin."

Andy said that the several ships being built in Germany for American President Lines were "post-Panamax"—too large for the Panama Canal—and were intended for runs in the Pacific. The latest Panamax ships were the so-called econs, or Econships, built in Korea for United States Lines and now owned by Sea-Land. "They are not ships but shit," Mac said. "They were made with a hammer and nail." Captain Ron Crook's Sea-Land Performance, which Andy had night-mated in Charleston, was an econ. Taking his work seriously, Andy had done his best to heed a sign on the bridge that said "CAUTION, DON'T WITHSTAND VOLTAGE & INSULATION RESISTANCE INSPECTION."

Mac picked up a piece of chalk and began writing cryptic numbers on the top of the steering selector. He could ignore the wheel, because the ship was on automatic pilot.

After adding, subtracting, erasing, multiplying, he said, "These hours have cashed in on my durability." He was computing his overtime.

Two-thirds of his work was overtime. There was required overtime, for dockings and undockings (handling the stern mooring lines), and most days he opted to work on deck for the bosun—chipping and painting—from nine to twelve in the morning and one to four in the afternoon. Weekends were pure overtime—on watch as on deck. His base pay was fifty-three dollars a day for a five-day, forty-hour week. But he wasn't working a five-day, forty-hour week; he was working fourteen to eighteen hours a day seven days a week. His hourly overtime rate was only thirteen dollars and seventy-eight cents, but there would be enough of it, he figured, to triple his base. In twelve weeks, he would earn about fourteen thousand dollars.

That is when I said, "This is a good watch."

And Mac said, "This is the *only* watch. The overtime watch. Sailors with the oldest shipping cards can name their watch. Nine out of ten prefer the four-to-eight. The early worm gets the bird."

It occurred to me that in being carried out to sea the word "overtime" had acquired enough special meaning to make it remarkably subtle. With its resonating nuances of opportunity and fairness, it created an entrepreneurial illusion among people who were actually working like ponies in a Scottish coal mine. Base pay or extra pay, it was all pay. Basic time or overtime, it was all time. With aggressive self-interest, with rewarded dedication, with nothing better to do, you willingly worked an eighty-hour week, worked eighteen hours on some days, for—as your chalk or your calculator would quickly tell you—about ten bucks an hour.

This, of course, had occurred to Mac, too. He said, "The only one who makes a decent salary is the bosun. It's chalk and cheese between my salary and his."

In the payoff port—Charleston, Newark, or wherever—an armored car drives up to the gangway, and the crew is paid in cash.

For the unlicensed deckhands, overtime is almost a synonym for chipping rust. It begins after breakfast. Mac, Calvin, Peewee, and others report to the shelter deck, where the bosun disperses jobs. Chipping rust is a job for people made of neurological nylon. They use hand-held jackhammers—needle guns, chisel guns, Bumble Bees, triple scalers. They dislodge rust and they create sound. Wherever they are, wherever you are, you can hear them. You can climb the flying bridge, wrap a pillow around your ears, stuff yourself in a hawsepipe, hide under a table—you cannot escape the sound. As a result, there are union rules limiting the sound to six hours a day. Depending on where you are, the chippers can seem to be hovering aircraft, they can seem to be splashing water, they can suggest a dentist drilling in a cavity hour after hour. There is a rust buster so large, so heavy, so lurchingly difficult to control that Vernon McLaughlin is often the only sailor willing to accept the task. This is the Arnessen Horizontal Deck Scaler, colloquially known as the lawnmower. It looks something like a lawnmower, but if it were ever used on a lawn it would bury itself in seven seconds. After standing watch from four to eight, Mac will run the lawnmower from nine to twelve and again from one to four, while Peewee follows him, sweeping chips. They wear masks. One day years ago, when Mac was on a C-2 called the Flower Hill, he was hanging over the side with a hand-held Arnessen hammer. The machine went right through the hull. Mac filled the hole with Red Hand epoxy putty.

The chipping opportunities offered by the Stella Lykes are reminiscent of the Flower Hill. Owned first by Moore-McCormack and later by United States Lines, Stella was in mothballs in Jacksonville for a year and a half before Lykes Brothers took her over. She was not well maintained. Duke the Bosun Labaczewski will guide you around the main deck from valley to valley of ulcerated rust. "It is made by water laying steady," he says. "The lawnmower doesn't get all of it. After that, you have to use the triple scaler and the needle gun. The needle gun gets right into the pits." All this, and the painting that follows, Duke directs from the shelter deck—a name borrowed from tankers and applied here to a room on the main deck that reaches from one side of the ship to the other and has large doors at either end that open to views of the ocean. It is a tunnel through the ship with breezes at the extremes. If you go into the shelter deck when the ship is rolling, you see sky at one end, water at the other. The shelter deck is full of ladders, hoses, cables, cargo lights, rigs of block and tackle, turnbuckles, rope, and, above all, paint—the whiff of paint.

After fo'c'sle deck and fantail, it's the most nautical space aboard, and seems to smell of creosote and tar.

I like to hang about the shelter deck talking to Duke. He is from New Jersey, and he makes me feel at home. Like his A.B.s and his ordinaries, he is at home not only with hand-held jackhammers but also with clove hitches, running hitches, sheet bends, and bowlines. Of marlinspike seamanship there may not be a great deal left on the oceans, but you will find it in the shelter deck.

Duke is short and muscular and wears a puffy white hat. He grew up in Camden and Philadelphia, where one of his close friends was a boy named Mike Perlstein. In 1947, when Duke was eighteen—and a veteran of the North Atlantic in the wartime Merchant Marine—Perlstein told him about Aliyah Bet, the secret Jewish effort to lease or buy ships, clandestinely load them with displaced European Jews, and take them to Palestine. The ships were very old, and the crews were not paid. Duke volunteered. He sailed on a ship called Hatikvah, a former Coast Guard cutter, which crossed the ocean in ballast and then replaced the ballast with fourteen hundred Jews. Duke was one of two Gentiles on the ship. The other was Hugh McDonald, a Harvard law student. McDonald painted a shamrock on the Hatikvah's stack.

"A *shamrock!*" I exclaimed as the narrative reached this point.

Duke said, "He might have been Scottish, but he was a very well-educated man."

Like the Exodus and the nine other Aliyah Bet vessels that sailed from America in 1946 and 1947, the Hatikvah failed to penetrate the British blockade. Fifty miles off the coast, the Hatikvah was boarded. Its passengers and crew were interned on Cyprus. Eventually, Duke and everybody else made it to the Holy Land. In Haifa, the volunteers were provided with new clothing, which included a short-sleeved shirt. That embarrassed Duke, because his arms were covered with tattoos and he knew that Judaic tradition barred tattoos. Jewish officials went out and bought him a long-sleeved shirt. David Ben-Gurion heard this story. After Duke moved into the Kibbutz Genosar, David Ben-Gurion looked up the volunteers, and expressed astonishment that a Gentile would put himself out to such an extent for a Jewish cause. "I was young and idealistic," Duke explains. "I was trying to help these people have a homeland." Forty years later, Duke was invited to a reunion in Israel, which he attended with Yehuda Sela, Hillel Haramati, Menahem Peretz, Aryeh Malkin, Mike Perlstein, Paul Kaye, Murray Aronoff, Harry Weinsaft, Nat Nadler, Ben Ocopnick, Irving Meltzer, Yakov Ben-Yisrael, and other American sailors from the Aliyah Bet. Israel, in its gratitude, gave each sailor a medal, bearing the face of David Ben-Gurion.

Duke is highly skilled as a fly-fisherman and spin-fisherman and as a bow hunter. A widower for ten years, he lives with his daughter on the southern fringes of the Pine Barrens. He has two granddaughters. Their mother works. Every day that Duke is ashore, he combs the hair of the younger one before sending her off to school. Wherever he goes on the ocean, he buys jewelry boxes. He puts gold in them in the form of rings, earrings, and chains. At this time, each granddaughter has ten thousand dollars' worth of gold.

After we left Panama, Andy went around the house like the Ship Crier, knocking on doors and calling, "Sea watches are set. Get up if you want to work. Rise and shine for overtime." With all our dockings and undockings and ulcerated rust, an ordinary seaman on the Stella Lykes can make more than an A.B., or even the bosun on a tanker: witness Peewee's thirty thousand dollars last year. In addition to overtime, an A.B. gets five dollars and forty-seven cents an hour for not eating lunch, if mandatory work on deck keeps him away from the food. It's called penalty time. J. Peter Fritz, the chief mate, says, "They eat, work, and sleep, and stand their watch. They get off and laugh all the way to the bank." Peewee averages more than seven hours of overtime a day, Calvin and Mac about six and two-thirds. The chief cook made fifty thousand dollars last year. There is a daily bonus if explosives are aboard. It's sometimes called ammo pay. In the engine room, there is a dividend known as daily dirty work, paid at the discretion of the chief engineer to some demac, like David Carter, who will work inside a boiler at a hundred and fifty degrees. Carter earned forty-five thousand last year.

The mates are paid copious overtime. The chief mate seems to work around the clock, and—forty-two days on, forty-two days off—goes home with roughly seventy-five thousand a year. Andy's base pay is a hundred and one dollars and twenty-eight cents a day, his overtime rate twenty-six dollars and thirty cents an hour. He gets overtime pay for, among other things, climbing twelve feet up turnbuckles and lashings to look at thermometers and record the temperatures of refrigerated containers. Every morning after breakfast, he reads the reefers for an hour. Luke Midgett, his predecessor as second mate, grossed twelve thousand dollars in forty-two days.

On Mac's birthday, the ship itself was making money running slow, because we were ahead of schedule. Seventy-one revolutions per minute. Fifteen knots. Undertime. Even so, she was consuming a gallon of bunker fuel every five seconds, a barrel every three and a half minutes. Three hundred thousand dollars had bought enough fuel to get us from Charleston to Chile and back. Mac said, "When we get up to maximum speed is when she just drinking like water." The captain never goes higher than eighty-eight r.p.m., which makes about nineteen knots. Andy looked up from his weather reports, and his fingers began to tap a calculator. That would be fifty-nine gallons a mile, he told us—seventeen thousandths of a mile per gallon.

Calvin was hosing the flying bridge, and Peewee was mopping the wheelhouse floor—the ritual end of the watch. Calvin had a long-handled brush that reached down to the bridge windows. While the iron mike steered the ship, Mac, with a cloth and Windex, sprayed the glass from the inside. The ship makes its own fresh water, and in such abundance that the whole house can be washed, helping the paint to last.

Andy said that we had found the Humboldt Current. The sea temperature had dropped ten degrees, and the ship had been set (shoved) to starboard four miles in less than two hours. Captain Washburn said that the Spaniards had not had the seamanship to sail against "the old Humboldt." He said it took them three months to go from Panama to Lima. "They even tried rowing. They never mastered the use of sail, the way the English did. The English had to. Up there, you mastered the use of sail or you died."

The chief mate appeared for the eight-to-twelve. Victor Belmosa relieved McLaughlin at the wheel. "Don't hit a porpoise," someone said to him.

Belmosa said, "Straight between the anchors."

Mac, to greet his fifty-ninth year, gave himself a birthday present. He did not turn out for overtime. He went to his cabin and slept all day.

We left fifteen thousand seven hundred and twenty-eight GAZ lighters on the dock in Valparaiso. We left four tons of mattress ticking, twelve tons of scouring pads, and two tons of books. We left fatty acid, silicic acid, nalidixic acid, polyvinyl-chloride resin, hexane, methane. We left eighteen thousand pounds of cellophane. We left eight pails of "flammable flavoring extracts," which, according to the cargo manifest, had a "flash point of 32 degrees Fahrenheit" and were "licensed by the United States for ultimate destination Chile and for distribution or resale in any destination except Soviet bloc, Laos, Libya, North Korea, Kampuchea, or Cuba." We left one container said to contain "sausage casings, water filters, auto parts, paper-making-machinery parts, and safety equipment—mixed," and another container said to contain "spare parts for front-end loader, paper-making machinery, aircraft parts, fluorescent tubes, valves, plastic film, air-conditioning parts, and epoxy catalysts." We left thirteen thousand pounds of sunflower seeds and twenty-five thousand pounds of alfalfa seeds. We left three hundred and sixty-four cases of hypodermic syringes that we had picked up in Colombia. We left a hundred and sixteen tons of steel strapping and (in Chile!) nine tons of copper wire. We left a ton and a half of money-changing machinery, forty-three tons of used clothing, a Model 1080 crane crawler, and a fire engine. Among other things.

We picked up three thousand cases of wine, two tons of button-down short-sleeved shirts, seven hundred bags of pentaerythritol, three hundred and fifty pounds of Chilean bone glue, and a hundred and thirteen thousand pounds of candy. We picked up eight hundred and seventeen desks and eight hundred and seventeen chairs. We picked up eighty-five cartons of umbrellas (on their way to Los Angeles), seven thousand spare tires (New Orleans), six thousand four hundred and eighty toilet pedestals (Chicago), and a hundred thousand pieces of kiln-dried radiata pine (destinations everywhere). We picked up nine tons of fruit cocktail, sixty-three tons of peach chips, sixty-seven tons of raisins, two hundred and thirty thousand gallons of concentrated apple juice, four hundred thousand fresh lemons, four hundred thousand fresh onions, five hundred thousand fresh apples. And then we departed.

And now it is 4 A.M., cool, in the fifties, northbound, and the lights of Valparaiso go into the ocean behind us. The onions are in six abovedeck containers. The onions need air, and the doors of the containers have been left open. The aroma emerges like smoke. It thins in the wind, but some of it streams past the bridge. This is a night so dark and clear that Venus is lighting a path on the water. A broad, bright path on the water. If you look directly at Venus, you dent your retinas—you look away and see a purple planet. Andy has seen rainbows made by the moon.

The shaft is making sixty revolutions a minute as the captain continues his slow economical trudge across the weekend to Peru. The ship, scarcely making fourteen knots, is all the more vulnerable to the big Pacific swells. The rolls are long and deep. She creaks like a bark in the doldrums. When Vernon McLaughlin takes over the wheel, he says, "I'd rather be in port than out here rolling around. If you were going to North Europe, you wouldn't be drifting around like this. You'd get up and be going, and hope to God the weather didn't catch you."

Dawn begins. It backlights the Andes. In day after day of overcast, we have not seen them before.

"Holy Toledo, look at those mountains, Mac. What do you say to that?"

"You can never please a seaman."

If the Fathometer were capable of registering awe, awe is what it would register now. While we are watching the mountain ridgeline, the machine is looking under the ship. On its electrolytic paper, the steep jagged sketch of the continental slope looks like cartoon lightning. The mountains rise beyond twenty-two thousand feet to the greatest elevation in the Western Hemisphere. The ocean close to the continent is as deep as the mountains are high. This trench—the Peru-Chile Trench—runs the length of South America. A few hundred miles north of us, near Antofagasta, it is twenty-six thousand feet deep. The abyssal plains of the world ocean floors are not nearly as deep as that. Like the Cayman Trench, the Peru-Chile Trench is a phenomenon of plate tectonics. It is the site of a plate-to-plate collision. South America, moving west, is encountering the ocean-crustal rock of the Nazca Plate, which plunges eastward under the continent. Each increment of this motion is an earthquake. Each volcano is in part the product of melted ocean crust.

A geologist might say:

> It is hardly possible to doubt that this great elevation
> has been effected by successive small uprisings . . . .
> by an insensibly slow rise.

The pried-up edge of South America is like a partly submerged cliff. As we move north with our toilet pedestals, our spare tires, and our two tons of button-down shirts, we are halfway up a ten-mile rise, ruffling the boundary of two fluids.

> Daily it is forced home on the mind of the geologist,
> that nothing, not even the wind that blows, is so un-
> stable as the level of the crust of this earth.

The dawn is pink behind Mercedario, orange and pink behind Aconcagua. The range is black. There is a thin line of bright silver where the ridges intersect the sky.

> Every one must have remarked how mud-banks, left by the retiring tide, imitate in miniature a country with hill and dale; and here we have the original model in rock, formed as the continent rose during the secular retirement of the ocean.

The geologist is Charles Darwin, and those are descriptions of Chile, where he experienced an earthquake that was the most severe in local memory.

> I happened to be on shore, and was lying down in the wood to rest myself. It came on suddenly, and lasted two minutes, but the time appeared much longer. The rocking of the ground was very sensible.

He felt a little giddy when he stood up.

> It was something like the movement . . . felt by a person skating over thin ice, which bends under the weight of his body. A bad earthquake at once destroys our oldest associations: the earth, the very emblem of solidity, has moved beneath our feet like a thin crust over a fluid.

Darwin described a tsunami as well, and, by intuition, understood its behavior:

> I suspect (but the subject is a very obscure one) that a wave, however produced, first draws the water from the shore, on which it is advancing.

He described the mountains. By a leap of the intellect that seems to me to have gone far beyond intuition, he understood what made them:

> In all probability, a subterranean lake of lava is here stretched out. . . . We may confidently come to the conclusion that the forces which slowly and by little starts uplift continents, and those which at successive periods pour forth volcanic matter from open orifices, are identical. From many reasons, I believe that the frequent quakings of the earth on this line of coast are caused by the rending of the strata, necessarily consequent on the tension of the land when upraised, and their injection by fluidified rock.

Having Darwin for a guide—to people and places as well as rock—is a bright fringe of this voyage. Especially when he was young, he was such a clear, good-humored writer.

> Whoever called "Valparaiso" the "Valley of Paradise" must have been thinking of Quillota.

> The Chilian miners are a peculiar race of men in their habits. Living for weeks together in the most desolate spots, when they descend to the villages on feast-days, there is no excess or extravagance into which they do not run. They sometimes gain a considerable sum, and then, like sailors with prize-money, they try how soon

> they can contrive to squander it. They drink excessively, buy quantities of clothes, and in a few days return penniless to their miserable abodes, there to work harder than beasts of burden. This thoughtlessness, as with sailors, is evidently the result of a similar manner of life.

> These lizards, when cooked, yield a white meat, which is liked by those whose stomachs soar above all prejudices.

He wrote the sort of thing that can give other writers ideas. The seminal aspects of his work may have extended beyond science.

> By the middle of the day we arrived at one of the suspension bridges made of hide, which crosses the Maypu, a large turbulent river a few leagues southward of Santiago. These bridges are very poor affairs. The road, following the curvature of the suspending ropes, is made of bundles of sticks placed close together. It was full of holes, and oscillated rather fearfully, even with the weight of a man leading his horse.

He was twenty-five when he reached Chile. He had a geological hammer, and he knew what he was hitting. He did not so much bring his geology with him, though, as figure it out in mid-terrain. The science in its modern form was less than forty years old. Plate tectonics, as a term coined to describe a theory, was a hundred and thirty-three years away. Yet he went through the country in 1834 decoding the message written in the stratified shingle. The presence of seashells at thirteen hundred feet did not suggest to him the flood of Noah. Darwin saw the stratigraphy, comprehended the structure, and understood most of the tectonics. And as far as he went he was right.

> No one fact in the geology of South America interested me more than these terraces of rudely-stratified shingle. . . . I am convinced that the shingle terraces were accumulated, during the gradual elevation of the Cordillera, by the torrents delivering, at successive levels, their detritus on the beachheads of long narrow arms of the sea, first high up in the valleys, then lower and lower down as the land slowly rose. If this be so, and I cannot doubt it, the grand and broken chain of the Cordillera, instead of having been suddenly thrown up, as was till lately the universal, and still is the common opinion of geologists, has been slowly upheaved in mass.

In the heavy roll, Stella's bridge wings alternately reach for the water, like the hands of a swimmer. Captain Washburn enters the wheelhouse. His belt buckle is stationed at his left hip today. There are days when the buckle is on his right hip. It is rarely in the middle. When we are not in port, he wears thinly striped semitransparent sports shirts, long dark trousers, running shoes. Always, he wears the baseball cap with the scrambled eggs. He says, "A quartering wind makes a ship roll."

McLaughlin, without expression, looks straight ahead. One does not need a Fathometer to sense what Mac is thinking. Let's get on with it, he is thinking. If you were in the North Atlantic, you wouldn't be drifting around like this.

The captain mentions Columbus. Captain Washburn would be unlikely to include Columbus on any list that also included Clean Shirt George Price, Dirty Shirt George Price, and Terrible Terry Harmon. "Columbus was a great big con man," he says. "Columbus knew where he was going and what was there. He thought it was closer—that was his mistake. He became nervous when he didn't find it. The men said they were turning back. Columbus said, 'Not all of you are turning back. The ones I kill are staying here.' " With a pugilistic frown, Washburn looks around the bridge.

Columbus sailed with fifty-two men on a square-rigger that was a hundred and seventeen feet long. Washburn is sailing with thirty-three on a merchant ship that is six hundred and sixty-five feet long. Washburn calls this undermanning. Steaming between the Scylla of automation and the Charybdis of bankruptcy, contemporary American shipping companies find ways to get along without crewmen: they beach the purser, the second cook, the sous-chef, the extra third mate, a wiper or two, and various engineers. Many ships larger than the Stella Lykes have scarcely twenty men aboard. If you are looking for large crews, you would look to a navy. Darwin's little warship had a crew of sixty-five. A modern United States Navy frigate, barely half the size of the Stella Lykes, will have two hundred and fifty men aboard, seven of them rubbing shoulders at any one time on the bridge.

When Darwin got off H.M.S. Beagle in Valparaiso, he was ashore nearly four months. When we got off the Stella Lykes in Valparaiso, we were ashore scarcely six hours before the longshoremen had loaded the button-down shirts, and the ship was preparing to go. The crew members do not see much of the countries they come to. Andy, who was so pleased to be making a run for the first time to the west coast of South America, could not get off in Cartagena or in Guayaquil and had time in Balboa only for a short walk with me. In Guayaquil, the ship was moved from one berth to another at noon, and he had to be aboard for that, and then at four he went on watch, and then we sailed. In the old days of the stick ships, turnaround time was long. A ship would sit in port a week or two. With the innovation of container ships and heavy-lift sheer-leg dockside cranes, the handling of cargo became intensely efficient. Our port visits are so brief that we often stay on sea watches. If port watches were set, a mate, for example, would be eight hours on and eight off, then eight more on and eight off, and then have thirty-two hours to himself. By that time, the Stella Lykes would be at least halfway to the next country. In the forty-two days of a voyage, J. Peter Fritz, the chief mate, who is in charge of cargo, usually goes ashore twice, and only briefly. The captain goes ashore even more rarely. When he comes up the gangway in Charleston to begin his routine of two voyages, he figures that the next time he sets foot on land will be eighty-four days later, in the same place. Andy was once on a dry-cargo ship that was in port a week at a time, but since then he has seldom been in any port more than twenty-four hours. Join the merchant navy and glimpse the world. Glimpse, in fact, only the seaports of the world. I heard a crewman say, "You get to Haifa, you can't get to Jerusalem. You get to Alexandria, you can't get to Cairo."

In some ways, we may be better off not getting much of anywhere. We have books and pamphlets aboard that warn of the hazards of South America, none in such replete fashion as Rand McNally's "South American Handbook," which is the definitive compilation in its field and is published in England. With respect to peril, the places we visit stand high in this book. It ranks Ecuador, Colombia, and Peru as countries where a traveller would be justified in feeling least secure. Intended for readers who have decided to expend large amounts of time, money, and energy on journeys in South America, it is a sort of welcome mat with land mines in it. Something seems to explode from almost every page:

> Always carry your passport with you; if it is not in your possession you may be taken to prison.
>
> You can be fined on leaving the country for staying too long.

Don't get into . . . conversations . . . with any locals if you can help it.

Beware of locals who smear mustard (or something worse) on you, and while you are cleaning it off, steal your belongings.

Beware of armed robbery; at roadblocks it is best not to get out of your car.

Be especially careful of people who describe themselves as plain-clothes police.

Never accept food, drink, sweets or cigarettes from unknown fellow-travelers on buses or trains. They may be drugged, and you would wake up hours later without your belongings.

Mugging, even in daylight, is a real threat.

Hide your main cash supply.

Take spare spectacles.

Try not to resist.

Don't pick up money in the street; it is often a ruse to rob you.

Avoid staying in hotels too near to bus companies, as drivers who stay overnight are sometimes in league with thieves.

Robbery is common on the beaches and you are advised to sit on your clothes.

You shouldn't take a taxi which has 2 people in it as you may get mugged or robbed.

We have received reports of drug-planting . . . on foreigners in Lima, with US$500 demanded for release.

The activities of the "maoist" guerrilla movement, Sendero Luminoso, are spreading. . . . They have no love for foreign tourists.

Travel in the departments of Ayacucho, Apurímac, and Huancavelica . . . is hazardous as there are many police and troops in the area fighting guerrillas and detaining suspects.

Tourists in the Callejón de Huaylas have been attacked, not so much by local people, but particularly by dogs.

There are excellent hospitals in both Quito and Guayaquil.

Many people have been badly poisoned by eating the blue berries which grow near the lake; they are *not* blueberries, they render the eater helpless within 2 hrs.

Milk . . . is rarely pasteurized and, therefore, a source of tuberculosis, brucellosis, and food-poisoning germs. This applies equally to ice-cream, yoghurt and cheese.

Stand your glass on the ice cubes rather than putting them in the drink.

Locals sell necklaces made with red and black Rosary Peas (Abrus pecatorius), which are extremely poisonous.

Rabies is endemic throughout Latin America so avoid dogs that are behaving strangely, and cover your toes at night to foil the vampire bats.

Sailors have returned to the Stella Lykes clothed only in their undershorts. The muggers peel them like bananas.

Glimpses of Guayaquil: Heavy construction, bamboo scaffolding . . . Rubber trees in the medians of streets . . . Shrimp cocktails in double goblets—the cooked shrimp in a glass sphere, surrounded by live, swimming fish . . . A checkerboard on a bicycle seat—a game being played with bottle caps, half of them upside down . . . In the heart of the city, the perched iguanas high in the branches of trees . . . The four clocks of the cathedral towers, each agreeing with the others, all correct twice a day. In the broad savannas across the Guayas, dark beans drying in the sun, green bananas beside the road. Papayas. Pineapples. Mangoes. Cane. The shrubs of coffee. The evergreen cacao. Billboards warning of "DROGADDICCIÓN." A clear-plastic bag of what appears to be gazpacho hanging from the handlebars of a policeman's motorcycle. Since the ship sails in two hours, it is time to return to the ship.

Glimpses of Valparaiso: Men in topcoats, women in fur-lined boots, the leafless trees, the dank English air, the February aspect of August . . . Grandmothers chewing bubble gum . . . As the hills go up, values go down. The streets are ever poorer as they rise. Darwin:

> The town is built at the very foot of a range of hills, about 1600 feet high, and rather steep. . . . The rounded hills, being only partially protected by a very

scanty vegetation, are worn into numberless little gullies, which expose a singularly bright red soil.

The gullies, still numberless, are lined with houses, each one higher and simpler than the last, grading upward into shacks. Halfway up the hill is a prison with a cracked wall. From the yard inside come the voices of prisoners singing in chorus. At elevation fifteen hundred feet, the door of a tin shack opens. A woman emerges who would not look amiss crossing a Fifth Avenue sidewalk to a stretch limo. She walks beside a gully on a dirt path to a street, where she waits for a bus. From sixteen hundred feet, the view is of two cities (Valparaiso and Viña del Mar) in amphitheatrical bays, Stella Lykes in the toy harbor.

In Ecuador, Duke Labaczewski buys panama hats. He says they are better hats than he could buy in Panama. They are made underwater. He takes them to New Jersey and gives them to priests. In Valparaiso, crewmen buy stuffed piranhas. In Lima, they buy framed tarantulas. They buy framed bats that have the wingspans of sharp-shinned hawks. They drink a cream soda called Inca Cola. They look into the faces of uniformed men and women in flak vests and riot gear who carry tear-gas guns and rifles. They watch the armored vehicles with the turret-mounted water cannons. They retreat to the seaport, Callao—to the Happy Landing Night Club, to Anna's, to the Loussiana Bar. In Guayaquil you will find them in Anita's.

Evening, August 11th. Twenty-nine degrees south. The end of the first clear day in more than a week. The watch concludes in darkness. Rigil Kentaurus and Hadar point to the Southern Cross. At sea or ashore, of all our hurried glimpses here in the southern ocean, this is the most moving—this small, elegant assemblage of four proportional stars. They form a perfect shape. They are so unprepossessing that the attention they attract will not give way.

*

*   *

*

There is a long quiet on the bridge. It is finally broken by McLaughlin, speaking in the dark from the helm. He says, "One of the foreign ports where I never go ashore is Miami."

"Did you go ashore in Valpo, Mac?"

"I went ashore in Valpo."

"How far did you get?"

"To the first bar."

North through the night at thirteen knots doing ten-second rolls in the long Pacific swells.

Lying in your bunk, you can feel your brain sloshing back and forth. With your chin on your pillow and your arms spread, you are flying. Bank left. Bank right. Six banks a minute. As the ship heels, creaking, it sounds like a ratchet. Loose objects—"The Voyage of the Beagle," the "American Practical Navigator," the Casio HL-802 electronic calculator, the Seiko Quartz Snooze-Light alarm—have long since shot across the room, hit the walls, and fallen to the floor, where they move, and tumble against one another, like rocks in the bed of a stream. These big winter swells come all the way across the Pacific from New Zealand, six thousand miles, to close the ports of South America. They closed Valparaiso before we were there and will close it again within the week. And now we have come into the southeast trades. The wind, blowing on our starboard quarter, is perpendicular to the long swells, and the result is a confused sea.

On the bridge, before day, Calvin King's presence at the wheel is signed by the glow of his cigarette. Calvin seems to live on smoke. He stands steady, and seems not to notice any motion but the ship's heading. One assumes that if the ship were going down he would continue to inform the mate, in his slow Carolinian voice, "Three-four-one, three-four-one," until his drawl became a gargle. His thoughts this morning are on the foundering not of himself but of the United States Merchant Marine, and the absence of opportunity for young sailors. "An entry man now, he's looking at a lost cause," Calvin is saying. "To make a long arm short—the best I can sum it up—we just don't have any ships."

Vernon McLaughlin, by contrast, continues to be anything but oblivious of the rolling of the ship, of the turning of the shaft at a few revolutions per hour (or so it seems to him). As dawn passes, and he takes over as quartermaster, he says, "We are going backward. This is an ocean ship, rocking and creaking, and it's fucking monotonous." He is reminded of voyages across the Pacific. Like Calvin, though, he is physically steady on the moving deck. It does not concern him that the ship is trying to throw him over a bridge wing.

Likewise Andy. As the heavens fade, Andy has been out on the port bridge wing shooting Achernar, Mars, Sirius, and Venus—plucking them from the drift of clouds. Good with a sextant, he resembles a Castilian shepherd drinking wine. Ordinarily, he shoots the stars as an academic exercise, a way of keeping fresh his celestial navigation, which he figures out with his calculator and his dividers in the chartroom. As second mate, he enjoys his role as the ship's "navigator"—laying out courses on charts. However, the essence of the navigation has been purloined by the computer SatNav, which receives its intelligence from satellites. Some days ago, Andy said, "I almost wish the SatNav would bust down, so I could do something more challenging." This morning, he's got his wish. The SatNav's digital clock reads 10:08:19 Greenwich mean time. It has read 10:08:19 Greenwich mean time for two hours. As successive satellites have passed overhead, the SatNav has not accepted a fix. By taking fixes about once an hour, it ordinarily tells us, among other things, how far our next programmed way point is and where we are at the moment. In some places, such as the North Atlantic, there are redundant systems of electronic navigation—Decca, for example, in North Europe, in addition to loran and SatNav. A nervous ship may be using them all. Down here in the Southeast Pacific, SatNav is alone. Other electronic systems are not in place here, or anywhere near here. The SatNav includes a feature called automatic heading, but in fact it doesn't know what your heading is unless you tell it. Having shot the stars and now the rising sun, Andy knows where we are. He wants to tell SatNav, but he is unable to. Like a person whose cursor has ceased to blink, he is locked out of SatNav's keyboard. He has never before faced such a problem. He is speed-reading the SatNav manual. He, too, is impervious to the ship's roll. With his sextant, Andy could fix the horizon and shoot the sun from the bar of a flying trapeze.

Steaming south, when we did not see sun or stars from Guayaquil to Valparaiso, SatNav got us there. "If the SatNav is out and you can't use your sextant, you stay on dead reckoning," Andy remarks now. "You will see the coast on radar long before you hit anything. If the radar conks out, the problem becomes larger."

Captain Washburn arrives on the bridge, previously informed and unconcerned. He says he never uses SatNav anyway. Like Dirty Shirt George Price and Rebel Frazier, he has an instinct for dead reckoning—the deduced reckoning of one's position from recorded course and speed. He says, "Every once in a while, we have to tell SatNav, 'Hey, fool. We're over here.' "

SatNav, in its time, has been known to reciprocate. The development of satellite navigation has brought some embarrassment to the hydrographic charts of the world. For example, we happen at the moment to be on the "Pisco to Arica" chart of the waters of Peru and Chile, which dates to the British survey conducted in 1836 by Captain Robert Fitzroy, of the Beagle, with additions and refinements through 1958. As a result of satellite navigation, a large purple box has been added to this chart warning that a stretch of coastline near Punta del Infiernillo is almost two miles closer to Australia than its charted position. New York is where it thinks it is, but, until recently, if you looked at the chart of the "Gulf of Mexico and Caribbean Sea" you discovered that the entire island of Antigua was "reported to lie one and a quarter miles northward of its charted position." When Andrew Marvell, in the sixteen-fifties, reported that "the remote Bermudas ride in the ocean's bosom unespied," he was singing the song of SatNav, which showed that Bermuda was not in its charted position. Satellite measurements found that several of the Caroline Islands were misplaced by as much as three miles. Cartographers have had to move Africa.

Andy and the captain discuss their sextants—comparing their astigmatizers, their ability to pluck bodies out of clouds, their need to filter the brilliance of first-magnitude stars. This may be the only sextant shootout I will ever see. The captain admits to the difficulties he has when he tries to work with a bubble sextant but asserts that he can sense the horizon even if he can't see it. He says, "I've got a bubble inside my head that the rest of you guys don't have."

On merchant ships, they still marvel that John Wayne could read latitude and longitude right off his sextant on the bridge wing of a ship of the U.S. Cinemarine. Moreover, he did it on a cloudy day.

Andy likes to quote something he calls Higgins' Law, which comes off a wall at Maine Maritime: "USE ONE ELECTRONIC SYSTEM AND YOU ALWAYS KNOW WHERE YOU ARE. USE MORE THAN ONE AND YOU'RE ALWAYS IN DOUBT."

I have asked him if merchant ships can get along without celestial navigation.

"No" was his reply. "It's the one thing that doesn't rely on power. There is nothing else to fall back on when SatNav fails. Licensed deck officers don't really need to understand nautical astronomy, though. They just have to know how to do it. They don't need to know the constellations. They can use the sight-reduction tables for selected stars. You can shoot a star by looking first in the tables for its altitude and bearing. Then you set the sextant and shoot it."

The gyrocompass runs on power. The gyro informs the automatic pilot. Not only does the gyro have to be running; it has to be running properly. A merchant ship left Philadelphia for South America and ran aground on Long Island. When the ship was leaving Delaware Bay, the gyro evidently lost power and spun ever more slowly until it was at least ninety degrees in error. The power returned but the error remained. South became east, and north became west. The next day, the ship went aground in New York. Captain Washburn savors this story. "That was in the early nineteen-fifties," he says. "She started for South America and hit Fire Island. On the way, she went through three or four watches, and no one—no one, as in not one—checked the gyro against the magnetic compass. A gyro being as much as a hundred and eighty degrees off is not that uncommon. That story of the grounding on Fire Island is meant to show you, 'Hey, that gyro is just a machine and it can malfunction. Hey, check the equipment. Check that gyro with the magnetic repeatedly.' That is why they use that story in classes. Hey, if just one guy on one watch had checked that gyro against the magnetic and said, 'Hey, something's bad wrong here,' that wouldn't have happened. The ship went through at least three watches before it hit

Fire Island. All *three* watches were involved. When they were aground, they had no idea where they were."

Andy says, "The insidious thing is that so much of your equipment is calibrated to that gyro. As the gyro wanders off course, everything else wanders with it. So everything agrees. Everything checks out. Your autopilot will follow it around ever so slowly. Your course recorder won't show a change of course. Your radars will agree with it. Everything else will agree with that gyro."

Captain Washburn was leaving Charleston one time and had settled in his bunk for a nap when sunlight came streaming through his porthole. Given the hour and the ship's intended heading, sunlight coming through the porthole was about as alarming as a flood of green sea. In a few seconds, Washburn was on the bridge. "The gyro said ninety but it was really two-seventy, and we were heading back for Charleston," he says, continuing the story. "Meanwhile, the mate was up there leaning on his chin, you know, heading away from the sun, the ship turned all the way around, a hundred and eighty degrees, going back, you know, and all of this isn't registering. We were just starting the trip—and I'm supposed to go below and *sleep* with him on the bridge?"

In the eighteenth century and before, a ship's captain would almost always be the only person on the ship who could calculate the ship's position. He used the instruments and possessed the skills of navigation. The chronometer came into use in the seventeen-sixties. The sextant was invented in 1731. Cruder devices for measuring the angles between celestial bodies and the horizon—the astrolabe, the cross-staff—preceded the sextant. Whatever the instruments were, they were emblematic of the captain—the one person who could get the ship from A to C without veering off to G or wrecking it on B. This godlike knowledge helped to subordinate the crew and, if things went sour, to prevent mutiny. If you threw the captain overboard, who would get you home?

Nathaniel Bowditch, of Salem, Massachusetts, who was born in 1773, undertook to bring navigation out of the realm of mystery and into the understanding of ordinary seamen. His first pupil was himself. He did not go to school beyond the age of ten. He went to sea at twenty-one. He was the skipper of a merchant ship before he was thirty. He taught his sailors math. He taught them navigation. Like every other ship's master, he used John Hamilton Moore's "The Practical Navigator" as a text, but after he had found and corrected eight thousand errors in Moore's book he rewrote it completely and, in 1802, published it under his own name. This became the "American Practical Navigator," subtitled "An Epitome of Navigation." There is one on every Navy ship, one on every merchant ship—a copy in the chartroom of the Stella Lykes. The book has long since been taken over by the Defense Mapping Agency of the Department of Defense and is continually revised. Universally, it is known as Bowditch. It is two thousand pages long, includes vastly more than how to get from A to C, and, from its star charts to its discussion of relative bearings, is the Britannica of the sea. If John Wayne had known what he was doing, he would have put down the sextant, picked up a pencil, and referred to the tables in Bowditch.

Andy Chase owns Nathaniel Bowditch's sextant. This is not the sort of thing he is likely to confide to the captain. When Andy goes on ships, he doesn't take it with him. He takes another. He leaves the heirloom at home and will someday present it to a museum. I stumbled across this curious fact when Andy was trying to teach me how to use a sextant, and I was looking for the angle of Mimosa, a star of the Southern Cross. There were aspects of Andy's background that had long puzzled me. For example, he had studied in a New England prep school, just about the last milieu one would imagine as a nursery for the Merchant Marine. Yet he took off from the school and shipped out on a bulk carrier. One of his grandfathers was a professor of history at Harvard. To be sure, when Andy was born his father was running a boatyard on Long Island Sound, and he later worked for a tuna company and flew the world as a sort of water-pack diplomat, visiting the tuna industries of numerous countries. But, for all that, I was struck by the apparent paradox between the fabric of Andy's origins and the romantic profundity of his attachment to the sea. And I remained so until this morning, when I was trying to hold the bright Mimosa in the index mirror of the sextant, and he told me about the priceless old sextant at home, and explained that it was there because Nathaniel Bowditch was his great-great-great-grandfather. On page 3 of the current edition of the "American Practical Navigator" a naval historian says that Bowditch learned more than twenty languages in order to be able to acquire the navigational knowledge that he passed along to American sailors. When Andy called at Leningrad on the Waterman freighter Thomas Jefferson, he studied the names on Russian ships from the launch that carried him ashore. The names generally appeared twice—in both Roman and Cyrillic characters. Before the launch reached the dock, Andy had figured out the Cyrillic alphabet, and he was able to get around in the city on buses. In common with numerous sailors on the Stella Lykes, Andy has a tattoo on his right forearm. Off the bulk carrier Kristin Brøvig, he went ashore near Sydney, aged sixteen, and looked around for a parlor. He explains that he chose to do this where he did for "the pure sound" of the word "Australia"; that is, it would never do to be tattooed in a place like Scranton. "It was a romantic notion. I wasn't drunk. I wasn't impulsive. I damned well wanted a tattoo. My brother had a tattoo. Real sailors had tattoos. People tell me I'm supposed to regret it. Unless you're convinced you want it, you shouldn't do it. There ain't no turning back. I've never regretted it. I looked at the sketches all over the walls, and picked out the one that I wanted. It's a square-rigger coming over the horizon, coming out of the rising sun." When Andy was in his teens, he sailed five thousand miles working for his brother Carl, who was the skipper of a schooner called Nathaniel Bowditch.

Below the bridge deck is the boat deck, and on the boat deck is Captain Washburn's office. Nine A.M. I often sit here in the morning drinking coffee, reading manifests, and listening to him. "My house is your house," he says, and the remark is especially amiable in this eight-deck tower called the house. During the night, a planned avalanche occurred in the office. From seaport to seaport, papers accumulate on the captain's desk. "Paperwork has become the bane of this job," he says. "If a ship doesn't have a good copying machine, it isn't seaworthy. The more ports, the more papers. South American paperwork is worse than the paperwork anywhere else in the world but the Arab countries and Indonesia." Deliberately, he allows the pile on his desk to rise until a deep roll on a Pacific swell throws it to the deck and scatters it from bulkhead to bulkhead. This he interprets as a signal that the time has come to do paperwork. The paper carpet may be an inch deep, but he leaves it where it fell. Bending over, he picks up one sheet. He deals with it: makes an entry, writes a letter—does whatever it requires him to do. Then he bends over and picks up another sheet. This goes on for a few days until, literally, he has cleared his deck.

The roll that set off last night's avalanche was probably close to thirty degrees. In a roll that is about the same, my tape recorder shoots across the office and picks up the captain with Doppler effect. Retrieving it, I ask him, "How many degrees will Stella roll?"

"She'll roll as much as she has to. She'd roll fifty degrees if you'd let her—if she was loaded wrong—but normally she'll roll in the twenty-to-thirty-degree range. That's average for ships. It doesn't slow her down or hurt her. She is a deep-sea vessel, built for rough weather. We don't see much rough weather down here. We used to run this coast with the hatches open. That would be suicidal anywhere else. Every day, somewhere someone is getting it from weather. They're running aground. They're hitting each other. They're disappearing without a trace." Once, in a great storm, Terrible Terry Harmon said to Washburn, "Do you know how to pray?" When Washburn nodded, Harmon said, "Then try that. That's the only thing that's going to save us now."

Straightening up with a sheet of paper in his hand, Captain Washburn looks out a window past a lifeboat in its davits and over the blue sea. After a moment, he says, "I love going to sea. I do not love that sea out there. That is not my friend. That is my absolute twenty-four-hour-a-day sworn enemy." He shows me a map of maritime casualties. He also has back issues of the *Mariners Weather Log*, a publication of the National Oceanic and Atmospheric Administration that chronicles marine disasters throughout the world and features among its reported storms a "Monster of the Month." Nautical charts, such as the ones in use in our chartroom, include a surprising number of symbols denoting partially submerged wrecks and completely submerged wrecks. Nearly all the ships that appear on modern charts have been wrecked in the past fifty years. "Here's a handsome ship went down," the captain continues, with a finger on his map. "She just went out and was never heard from again. So it isn't just these little nondescript ships like In God We Trust that disappear. Almost every hour of every day someone is getting it. Right now someone is getting it somewhere."

A likely place is a foul sea about eight hundred miles north of Hawaii that is known to merchant seamen as the Graveyard of the North Pacific. "You can pick it up on the shortwave," Washburn says. "You hear, 'SOS. We're taking on water. SOS. We're taking on water.' Then you don't hear the SOS anymore." There are weather-routing services that help merchant ships figure out where to go. Washburn suggests that they are in business not to provide maximum safety or comfort but to shave as close as they dare to vicious weather and thus save time and fuel. He happened to be visiting the home office of one of these services when it had a client in the Graveyard of the North Pacific and was guiding it between two storm systems. He wondered what might happen if the storms coalesced. He asked why such ships did not go past Hawaii on a route that has proved safe for four hundred years. The weather-routers said, "Then who would need *us*?"

When Washburn was a teen-age ordinary seaman, he sailed with a master who had written what Washburn describes as "a big sign inside the logbook":

TAKE CARE OF THE SHIP AND
THE SHIP WILL TAKE CARE OF YOU

The sign now hangs in Washburn's head. In his unending dialogue with the ship, the ship tells him things that its instruments do not. There is no Weatherfax map on the Stella Lykes—only the barometer, the barographs, the teletypes from NOAA. The radar can see a storm, but that is like seeing a fist just before it hits you. When a storm is out there, somewhere, beyond the visible sky, the ship will let him know.

"When you get close to a big storm, you can feel it. For some reason, the ship takes on almost a little uncertainty. She's almost like a live thing—like they say animals can sense bad weather coming. Sometimes I almost believe a ship can. I know that doesn't make sense, because she's steel and wood and metal, but she picks up a little uncertainty, probably something that is being transmitted through the water. It's hard to define. It's just a tiny little different motion, a little hesitancy, a little tremble from time to time."

Off Hatteras, things can be really hesitant. A lashed-down crane will pull a pad eye out of the deck. A pad eye is a D ring made of steel two inches thick. "This ship is very strongly built," Washburn says. "She's sturdy and reliable. There's lots of horsepower down there. She will answer the rudder. She will respond. She's a capable and trustworthy ship. You know what she'll do and you know her limitations. They aren't crucial, but you can't expect her to do things where you know she's a little short. You can't suddenly demand that of her and expect to get it. It isn't there. She's American-built. There's good steel in the hull. Those frames are close together. She'll roll on a following sea, but she's got a high-raised fo'c'sle head and a sharp bow. She's built for rough weather. She's built for rough handling. She's built to take seas and fight back. You cannot overpower seas. But she can deal with what's out there. She was built to go to Scandinavia in the middle of winter."

To make the North Europe run in winter is something that many American sailors do everything they can to avoid and others just refuse to do. No matter how straitened they may be and hungry for work, they will pass up the winter North Atlantic. Having grown up near this ocean and knowing no other, I was surprised to learn this. Years ago, when I was a student for a time in Europe and went back and forth on ships in winter, I thought it was normal for the keel to come out of water as the hull prepared to smash the sea. I didn't know anything about load lines—Plimsoll marks—or classification societies. For a ship to thud like a ton of bricks and roll at least forty degrees seemed a basic and expectable standard condition. I had no idea that this ocean in winter was in a category of its own. On various ships on the North Europe run, Captain Washburn has stayed awake for as much as seventy-two hours, catnapping in a chair on the bridge. "You're tacking into weather," he explains. "Winds and seas can become so strong that you can't always go in the direction you want to." For more than four years, he was the skipper of the Ro/Ro Cygnus and most of its runs were to North Europe. In the early weeks of 1983, he was trying to make his way north into the English Channel, but the Cygnus's big diesels were overmatched, overwhelmed. Washburn tacked back and forth almost helplessly, and the ship—five hundred and sixty feet, fourteen thousand deadweight tons—was blown sideways into the Bay of Biscay. "We couldn't get out. We ended up near Bilbao."

On the side of a merchant ship is a painted circle, a foot in diameter, with a horizontal line running through it marking the depth to which the ship can be safely loaded in summer. Near it are shorter horizontal lines, more or less like the rungs of a ladder. They indicate the depth to which the ship can be safely loaded in various seasons and places. The highest line, representing the heaviest permissible load, is marked "TF." Tropical fresh. This means that you can go up a river in the tropics to a place like Guayaquil, load yourself down to the TF line, and go back to the ocean, where the density of the water will lift the ship to another line, marked "T." That is as deeply loaded as you are permitted to be in a tropical ocean. These levels, worked out specifically for each ship, "take into consideration the details of length, breadth, depth, structural strength and design, extent of superstructure, sheer, and round of beam," and are collectively called the Plimsoll mark, after Samuel Plimsoll, a member of Parliament who, in the eighteen-seventies, wrote the act creating them in order to outlaw the greed-driven excessive loading that was the primary factor in the sinking of ships. When British people call rubber-soled deck and tennis shoes plimsolls, they are referring to him. The United States adopted the Plimsoll mark more than fifty years later. Load lines are set by classification societies, which are private companies that play a checking, testing, and supervisory role in ship construction—services that are optional in the sense that if you don't sign up for them no one will insure your ship. Society initials appear on the hull of a ship as a part of the Plimsoll mark: the American Bureau of Shipping (AB), Lloyd's Register (LR), Bureau Veritas (BV), Germanischer Lloyd (GL), Norske Veritas (NV). Below the summer load line is a line marked "W." It marks the depth to which the ship can be safely loaded in winter. Some distance below that is the lowest line of all. It is marked "WNA." To burden a ship only to that line is to give it the lightest load in the whole Plimsoll series. The WNA line marks the maximum depth to which the ship can be safely loaded in the winter North Atlantic. Andy has remarked about a company that runs to Iceland, "If you get a ship on that line in the winter, you're going to get creamed and you know it." The North Sea, the Cape of Good Hope, Cape Horn, and the Gulf of Alaska are the stormiest waters in the shipping world after the winter North Atlantic.

The great-circle route between North Europe and New York bucks the storms of the upper latitudes. Captain Washburn likes to say that if you were to take two new ships and run one to North Europe via the Azores and the other to North Europe on the great circle, after a year you would have one new ship and one "damaged, beat-up ship." He continues, "If you go south and the weather comes after you, you can go on going south. If you go north and the weather comes after you, you have containers over the side and the crew in the hold chasing loose cargo. You—you are going nowhere."

While Vernon McLaughlin was on the American Legacy, her skipper tried to run to the north of a storm and ended up against Newfoundland in a Force 12 gale.

"For two days, the ship pounded as it pitched, and rolled forty; you looked out the sides in a trough, and it looked as if you were underwater. There was a great crack in the superstructure in front of the house. Containers were lost over the side. Others were stood against each other like swords when a marine gets married. One that broke open—shoes fell out of it for the rest of the voyage. On other ships, I have seen seamen fall on their knees and pray, they were so afraid."

While Andy was night-mating the Sea-Land Performance in Charleston, Captain Crook told me about a January crossing he had made years before on the great-circle route from the Virginia capes to the Strait of Gibraltar. "We hit the worst sea storm to hit the North Atlantic ocean in two hundred years," he said. "For fifty-two hours, the captain was on the bridge trying to save the ship. Speeding up in the trough to maintain control, slowing up just before the crest so he wouldn't pound the ship too hard. Waves tore the mast off. The bridge was a hundred and fifteen feet off the water. Waves went over us. The decks were solid ice. Whole tractor-trailers were washed over the side. A forty-five-ton truck-crane was loose on the deck like a battering ram. House trailers on the second deck were completely demolished. I was truly afraid." An ordinary seaman was on lookout on the bridge when the ship lurched and hurled him through the wheelhouse door onto the port-side bridge wing, where he slid on his back across ice and went through the railing. He grabbed the railing, hung on, and dangled above the monstrous sea. Crook went out and pulled him back.

Andy once said to me, "I love being up on the bridge when it's rough. I enjoy being on watch in rough weather. It's so impressive. It's spectacular. Huge seas. Strong winds. At some point, you cross from awe to terror. I haven't been at that point yet—the ultimate storm. It could change my attitude." Andy hasn't seen anything worse than a fifty-five-foot sea breaking over him when he was running coastwise on the Spray in the winter North Atlantic. "My height of eye was fifty-two feet off the water, and the water broke over the bridge and hit the radar mast. Water went down stacks into the engine room." Not enough water to change his attitude.

That wave was what the *Mariners Weather Log* calls an ESW, or Extreme Storm Wave—a rogue wave, an overhanging freak wave. Coincidence tends to produce such waves—for example, when the waters of colliding currents are enhanced by tidal effects in the presence of a continental shelf. Often described as "a wall of water," an Extreme Storm Wave will appear in a photograph to be a sheer cliff of much greater height than the ship from which the picture was taken. Captain Washburn calls it "a convex wave." He goes on to say, "You don't get up it before it's down on your foredeck. The center is above sixty feet high. You can't ride over the center. You *can* ride over the edge. A ship has no chance if the wave hits just right. It will break a ship in two in one lick. Because of the trough in front of it, mariners used to say that they fell into a hole in the ocean."

In the winter North Atlantic, the demac David Carter has oftentimes tied himself in his bunk after propping his mattress up and wedging himself against the bulkhead—to avoid getting thrown out and injured by a forty-five- or fifty-degree roll. He got his first ship after nearly everyone aboard had been injured. On one voyage, Carter had a big chair in his cabin that was "bouncing off the bulkhead like a *tennis* ball." In his unusually emphatic, italic way of speaking, he goes on, "Pots won't stay on a *stove*. After a night of no *sleep*, a full day of *work*, you get nothing but a *baloney* sandwich if you're lucky. They soak the tablecloth so nothing will *slide*. I hope you won't get to see that. If you wonder why we *party* and get *drunk* when we're in port, that's why."

On February 11, 1983, a collier called Marine Electric went out of the Chesapeake Bay in a winter storm with a million dollars' worth of coal. She was a ship only about ten per cent shorter than the Stella Lykes and with the same beam and displacement. Our chief mate, J. Peter Fritz, wished he were aboard her. She was headed for Narragansett Bay, her regular run, and his home is on Narragansett Bay. He grew up there. As a kid, he used to go around on his bike visiting ships. He took photographs aboard the ships, developed and printed them at home, and went back with the pictures to show the crews. They invited him to stay aboard for dinner. ("Some guys liked airplanes. To me it was just the ships.") He watched the shipping card in the Providence *Journal*—the column that reports arrivals and departures. Working on a tug and barge, he learned basic seamanship from the harbormaster of Pawtuxet Cove—knots, splicing, "how to lay around boats the right way." As a Christmas present an aunt gave him a picture book of merchant ships. As a birthday present she gave him the "American Merchant Seamans Manual."

Peter grew up, graduated from the Massachusetts Maritime Academy, and went to sea. It was his calling, and he loved it. He also loved, seriatim, half the young women in Rhode Island. He was a tall, blond warrior out of "The Twilight of the Gods" with an attractively staccato manner of speech. Not even his physical attractions, however, could secure his romantic hatches. "Dear Peter" letters poured in after he left his women and went off for months at sea. Eventually, he married, had a son, and left the Merchant Marine. For several years, he worked for an electronic-alarm company and miserably longed for the ocean. ("I will not admit how much I love this job. The simple life. Having one boss. Not standing still, not being stagnant; the idea of moving, the constant change.") Eventually, he couldn't stand it any longer, and went off to circle the world on the container ship President Harrison. ("I had *the* killer card. I had planned it.") He made more money in eighty-seven days than he could make in a year ashore. After a family conference, he decided to ship out again. Like his lifelong friend Clayton Babineau, he coveted a job that would take him on short runs from his home port. Every ten days, the Marine Electric went out of Providence for Hampton Roads, and nine days later she came back. She went right past Peter's house. He night-mated her. His wife, Nancy, said to him, "Hey, wouldn't it be great if you got a job on that one? You could be home with your family." He tried repeatedly, without success. His friend Clay Babineau, sailing as second mate, died of hypothermia that night off Chincoteague in the winter storm. The Marine Electric was thirty-nine years old in the bow and stern, younger in the middle, where she had been stretched for bulk cargo. In the language of the Coast Guard's Marine Casualty Report, her forward hatch covers were "wasted, holed, deteriorated, epoxy patched." Winds were gusting at sixty miles an hour, and the crests of waves were forty feet high. As the Marine Electric plowed the sea, water fell through the hatch covers as if they were colanders. By 1 A.M., the bow was sluggish. Green seas began pouring over it. A list developed. The captain notified the Coast Guard that he had decided to abandon ship. The crew of thirty-four was collecting on the starboard boat deck, but before a lifeboat could be lowered the ship capsized, and the men, in their life jackets, were in the frigid water. In two predawn hours, all but three of them died, while their ship went to rest on the bottom, a hundred and twenty feet below, destroyed by what the Coast Guard called "the dynamic effects of the striking sea."

Peter Fritz, who gives the routine lectures on survival suits to the successive crews of the Stella Lykes, carries in his wallet a shipping card clipped from the February 13, 1983, Providence *Journal*: "ARRIVING TODAY, MARINE ELECTRIC, 8 P.M."

She is remembered as "a rotten ship." So is the Panoceanic Faith, which went out of San Francisco bound for India with a load of fertilizer about six months after Fritz graduated from Massachusetts Maritime. Five of his classmates were aboard, and all of them died, including his friend John McPhee. Getting to know Fritz has not been easy. There have been times when I have felt that he regarded me as a black cat that walked under a ladder and up the gangway, a shipmate in a white sheet, a G.A.C. (Ghost in Addition to Crew). The Panoceanic Faith developed a leak, its dampened cargo expanded, its plates cracked. It sank in daytime. "People tried to make it to the life rafts but the cold water got them first."

Plaques at the maritime academies list graduates who

have been lost at sea. A schoolmate of Andy Chase was on a ship called Poet that went out of Cape Henlopen in the fall of 1980 with a load of corn. She was never heard from again. Nothing is known. In Captain Washburn's words, "Never found a life jacket, never found a stick."

On the Spray, Andy went through one hurricane three times. A thousand-pound piece of steel pipe broke its lashings and "became the proverbial loose cannon." Ten crewmen—five on a side—held on to a line and eventually managed to control it, but they had almost no sleep for two days. The Spray once carried forty men. Reduced manning had cut the number to twenty. "Companies are trying to get it down to eleven or twelve by automating most functions," he says. "When everything's going right, four people can run a ship, but all the automation in the world can't handle emergencies like that."

A small ship can be destroyed by icing. Ocean spray freezes and thickens on her decks and superstructure. Freezing rain may add to the accumulation. The amount of ice becomes so heavy that the ship almost disappears within it before the toppling weight rolls her over and sinks her. Ships carry baseball bats. Crewmen club the ice, which can thicken an inch an hour.

To riffle through a stack of the *Mariners Weather Log*—a dozen or so quarterly issues—is to develop a stop-action picture of casualties on the sea, of which there are so many hundreds that the eye skips. The story can be taken up and dropped anywhere, with differing names and the same situation unending. You see the Arctic Viking hit an iceberg off Labrador, the Panbali Kamara capsize off Sierra Leone, the Maria Ramos sink off southern Brazil. A ferry with a thousand passengers hits a freighter with a radioactive cargo and sinks her in a Channel fog. A cargo shifts in high winds and the Islamar Tercero goes down with twenty-six, somewhere south of the Canaries. Within a few days of one another, the Dawn Warbler goes aground, the Neyland goes aground, the Lubeca goes aground, the Transporter II throws twenty-six containers, and the Heather Valley—hit by three waves—sinks off western Scotland. The Chien Chung sinks with twenty-one in high seas east of Brazil, and after two ships collide off Argentina suddenly there is one. A tanker runs ashore in Palm Beach, goes right up on the sand. The bow noses into someone's villa and ends up in the swimming pool. The Nomada, hit by lightning, sinks off Indonesia. The Australian Highway rescues the Nomada's crew. The Blue Angel, with a crew of twenty, sinks in the Philippine Sea. The Golden Pine, with a shifting cargo of logs (what else?) sinks in the Philippine Sea. A hundred and fifteen people on the Asunción drown as she sinks in the South China Sea. The Glenda capsizes off Mindanao, and seven of twenty-seven are rescued. The Sofia sinks in rough water near Crete, abandoned by her crew. The Arco Anchorage grounds in fog. On the Arco Prudhoe Bay, bound for Valdez, a spare propeller gets loose on the deck and hurtles around smashing pipes. The Vennas, with sixty-nine passengers and crew, sinks in the Celebes Sea. The Castillo de Salas, a bulk carrier with a hundred thousand tons of coal, breaks in two in the Bay of

Biscay. The container ship Tuxpan disappears at noon in the middle of the North Atlantic with twenty-seven Mexicans aboard. A container from *inside* the hold is found on the surface. Apparently, the ship was crushed by a wave. In the same storm in the same sea, a wave hits the Export Patriot hard enough to buckle her doors. Water pours into the wheelhouse. The quartermaster is lashed to a bulkhead so that he can steer the ship. In the same storm, the Balsa 24 capsizes with a crew of nineteen. In the Gulf of Mexico, off the mouth of the Rio Grande, fifteen Mexican shark-fishing vessels sink in one squall. In a fog near the entrance to the Baltic Sea, the Swedish freighter Syderfjord is cut in two in a collision and sinks in forty seconds. About a hundred miles off South Africa, the Arctic Career leaves an oil slick, some scattered debris, and no other clues. The Icelandic freighter Sudurland goes down in the Norwegian Sea. The Cathy Sea Trade, with twenty-seven, is last heard from off the Canary Islands. Off Portugal, the Testarossa sinks with thirty. Off eastern Spain, in the same storm, the cargo shifts on the Kyretha Star, and she sinks with eighteen or twenty. The Tina, a bulk carrier under the Cypriot flag, vanishes without a trace somewhere in the Sulu Sea. In a fog in the Formosa Strait, the Quatsino Sound goes down after colliding with the Ever Linking. In the English Channel, the Herald of Free Enterprise overturns with a loss of two hundred. The Soviet freighter Komsomolets Kirgizzii sinks off New Jersey. In the North Sea, the bridge of the St. Sunnivar is smashed by a hundred-foot wave. After a shift of cargo, the Haitian freighter Aristeo capsizes off Florida. On the Queen Elizabeth 2, Captain Lawrence Portet ties himself to a chair on the bridge. Among the eighteen hundred passengers, many bones are broken. Seas approach forty feet. After a series of deep rolls, there are crewmen who admit to fearing she would not come up. Off the Kentish coast with a hundred and thirty-seven thousand tons of crude, the tanker Skyron, of Liberian registry, plows a Polish freighter. The tanker bursts into flames. The fire is put out before it can reach the crude. Fifty-seven crewmen abandon two bulk carriers in the Indian Ocean. The Hybur Trader loses seventeen containers in a storm off Miami Beach. On the same day, off Fort Lauderdale, a Venezuelan crew of twenty-five abandons the container ship Alma Llanera. The Frio, out of Miami for Colombia, sinks off Yucatan. In the Gulf of Alaska, the Stuyvesant spills fifteen thousand barrels of Alaska crude. The Rolandia—twenty-seven hundred tons—capsizes off France. The Ro/Ro Vinca Gordon capsizes off the Netherlands. The Vishra Anurag, a cargo ship under the Indian flag, capsizes off Japan. A Philippine freighter capsizes, too, with forty thousand cases of beer. Somewhere, any time, someone is getting it.

Not every ship that goes down is destroyed by time or nature. Or by collision or navigational error. Crews have been rescued from lifeboats with packed suitcases and box lunches. Say South Africa needs oil desperately as the result of an embargo and is willing to pay at ransom rates. You disguise your supertanker by painting a false name, take it into a South African port to discharge the Persian crude, leave South Africa, open your skin valves to replace the oil with water, pack your suitcase, make your sandwiches, leave the valves open until the ship sinks. If you follow this scenario, you will win no awards for originality. Possibly you will collect insurance payments for the ship, and possibly for the "oil" that went down inside her. You may have to explain why there was no slick.

There is a lot of pentimento on the bows of the Stella Lykes. Former names are visible, even in fading light. The ship was built in 1964 and stretched in 1982. When she belonged to Moore-McCormack, she was called the Mormacargo. After Moore-McCormack died and United States Lines bought her, she became the American Argo. After United States Lines died, Lykes Brothers chartered her from financial receivers. Phil Begin, our chief engineer, has said, "We're operating someone else's ship. It's like a rental car. You don't want to come on here and spend a lot of money for one or two years. You want it to be safe and efficient but no more. You put up with irritations. You can't afford to scrimp and save, though. When you read about ships going down, that's what happens."

In Peter Fritz's letters home he avoids mentioning storms. He doesn't want to worry Nancy. On his long vacations, as he leans back, stretches his legs, and watches the evening news, a remark by a television reporter will sometimes cause him to sit straight up. To Peter it is the sort of remark that underscores the separateness of the American people from their Merchant Marine, and it makes him feel outcast and lonely. After describing the havoc brought by some weather system to the towns and cities of New England—the number of people left dead—the reporter announces that the danger has passed, for "the storm went safely out to sea."

McLaughlin in the evening as he steers the rolling ship: "There is a story in the Cayman Islands about a man who sailed downwind to fish. When the wind unexpectedly shifted, he sailed right back. People asked him, 'Did you catch any fish?' He said, 'Fair winds are better than fish.' "

Captain Washburn, whose belt buckle, like the sun, has shifted during the day from one hip to the other, mentions a Chilean freighter that went down not long ago with thirty-seven crewmen here in the winter swells. "But I've never been in a bad storm on this coast," he reaffirms. "They do happen, but it's like Hawaii, which has never been hit by a hurricane. In any kind of weather system, a thirty-degree roll is not uncommon. The biggest roll I've been in on any ship—that we measured—was fifty-three degrees. It tore things loose on that ship that had never been moved before. It tore out washbasins, desks were pulled loose from bulkheads. Everything on the ship was moving."

"Do you get seasick?" I ask.

"No."

"Have you ever been seasick?"

"Never a hint of it."

"Suppose Columbus had worked for Lykes Brothers. How would he have made out?"

"He probably wouldn't have operated all that well in a fleet situation. He did not produce. He was a maverick; he was an adventurer. Before he sailed, he knew the land was there. He knew of a place with a forty-foot tide. That could be only one place—the Bay of Fundy. I think he expected to discover a continent. He was not surprised at all that he did not find China—yet. He *thought* there was something else first. But this was meant to be not so much a voyage of exploration as a commercial venture. This was not Henry the Navigator just out to discover things. Hey, the people backing Columbus were after a new road to the riches of the Indies without this three-year trip all the way around Africa. They were after money. He tried to pacify them by taking a few Indians back, but he was continually in trouble with the backers, because he didn't show up with a ship full of riches. He was trying to tell them that anything will grow in the soils of the New World. He was trying to tell them, 'Hey, you can *colonize* this.' They weren't interested in colonizing anything. They weren't interested in growing coconuts and bananas and sending them back. They wanted spice, diamonds, jewels, furs, and gold—and he didn't produce. Columbus didn't produce, which is why he wound up in chains. He did not produce, and that was the bottom line. He was a maverick, an adventurer; he was not a follower of the party line. Come to think of it—not to compare myself with Columbus—some of those adjectives kind of fit me. But I did all right."

He has told me that he grew up near Walter Reed Hospital, in the Takoma Park section of the District of Columbia. His father, Daniel Webster Washburn, went off each day to the Veterans Administration, where he worked on the legal staff. Young Paul, in an impromptu manner, now and again took off for months at a time. Certain schools he attended were chosen not by him but for him: Fishburn Military School, Briarley Military Academy, the Y.M.C.A. Day School. For a few months, he also went to Roosevelt High School, and, for a few more months, to Central High School.

"My parents were probably requested to remove me from every school I went to as a youth. I didn't fit in."

Before Paul was born, his mother had lost a child.

"When I came along, and lived, she defended me against all comers. With a smirk and a smile, I walked away. Later in life, I gave that up hard."

He says he could make A in anything. If he wasn't interested, though, he didn't pass.

"I would start for school some mornings and not get there."

Aged thirteen, fourteen, and upward, he rode freights as a hobo. This was in the nineteen-thirties. Sometimes he took to the highways and hitchhiked, but he saw hitchhiking as a form of begging.

"Hitchhiking was asking someone for something, riding the rails was taking it. I would rather ride in a freight car than in the comfort of someone's automobile."

He would get on a moving freight even if he didn't know where it was going. He worked in a sheet-metal shop in Albuquerque for a few weeks, and moved on.

"It was time for me to go—why I don't know. I rode a friendly freight—a side-door sleeping car—to El Paso. In El Paso, you could sit on a park bench and, when you were ready to leave, get on the Southern Pacific. It ran through the park."

He remained on land but was not unmindful of the sea.

"Whenever I got close to water, I would sit there and watch anything that was floating."

For two months, he swung a sledgehammer as part of a Southern Pacific Railroad gang between Tucson and Yuma. Temperatures reached a hundred and ten degrees. The foreman died, and four others.

"I always asked for work, not food. Poor whites and blacks who had almost nothing were the first to share, and even offer. Affluent white neighborhoods called the police."

He stayed in some hobo jungles, but only briefly. His ideal home was an empty boxcar that had hauled hay or straw. He took coal from the tender and built a fire on the boxcar's wooden floor. He would wake up beside a hole in the floor with a smoking rim. To start fires, some hoboes used the lubricating dope from a train's axles. Captain Washburn never did that. If he couldn't find an empty boxcar, he would settle for the jaw head of a gondola. He rode in ice compartments at the ends of refrigerator cars when no ice was there. Sometimes he blinded a passenger train. Blinding a passenger train meant riding in the vestibule of the first car after the coal car. The site was far from ideal: there were stinging cinders in the wind, and if the train took on water he got soaked. He tied himself to tank cars with his belt to avoid being shaken off. The last resort was the top of a boxcar.

One night, when he was riding the Mobile, Montgomery & Western between Montgomery and Mobile, he saw a hotbox flaming. In rain and darkness, he crawled back over forty or fifty cars to reach the caboose, where he told two conductors about the hotbox. They stopped the train, separated the hotbox car, and put it on a siding. At this point in Captain Washburn's narrative, I expected him to tell me that the conductors called Bull Connor, who arrived with his Dobermans and took Washburn to the slammer. Actually, he spent the rest of that trip beside the stove in the caboose eating sandwiches. He was seventeen years old.

All over the United States, where the freights stopped he would go into city libraries and read books. Primarily, he read history.

"I was enveloped right into it."

He read biographies of Christopher Columbus. And

his favorite period was the century that followed. As he paces back and forth on the bridge, one can hear him speaking to himself of Raleigh, of Mary Queen of Scots, of, by his description, "the occupation of France, the early ship movements, the beginning of commerce, the establishment of the colonies—the Drakes, the Hawkinses, the Frobishers, the Davises." He tells it to the ship.

Away for as much as eight months at a time, Washburn would eventually return home, resume life in Takoma Park, try another school, and then, one day, head out again. During that era, Siebrand Brothers Great Three Ring Piccadilly Circus & Carnival Combined had a sideshow freak who walked barefoot over broken glass and could accommodate with impunity any amount of current from an electric chair. This was Paul Washburn. Siebrand Brothers Great Three Ring Piccadilly Circus & Carnival Combined was a truck show that made long stands in Southwestern cities. After a crowd had been collected in the sideshow, the barker introduced Washburn, saying, "And here we have a boy from Asia. He believes in a strange religion: he believes the more you torture the body, the quicker you go to Heaven. Sometimes he punctures his body with nails, needles, and knives. Tonight he walks on glass." When Washburn sat in the electric chair, his upper arms were strapped, and he held a light bulb in one hand. The switch was thrown. The bulb lighted. Any unbeliever who stepped up and touched Washburn received a terrific shock. He also did an "iron-tongue act." A weight was connected by a cord to a hook that appeared to pass through his tongue. He raised his head and lifted the weight.

He worked his way east with Cole Brothers Circus as a wagon hitcher. And when he happened to be in New Orleans he was—quite by accident—taken up by Ringling Brothers. He got into a dispute with the owner of what he remembers as "a greasy spoon on Canal Street," and the man threw him out the door. Washburn, describing himself, says, "I thought the kid was tough. I tried to fight back—a little fancy footwork, a sticking move." The man hit him so hard on the forehead that his nose bled for three weeks. A policeman intervened, and said to Washburn, "I know you. You're one of those rowdies from the circus." He dragged Washburn to the Ringling Brothers big top at the foot of Canal Street, and said to him, "Get back in there and stay there." Ringling Brothers gave him a job, and he stayed with the circus as it moved to Mobile and then Montgomery and Atlanta and Jacksonville. From Jacksonville, for the first time, he shipped out.

"I was down at the waterfront, and there was a banana boat going to the Dominican Republic—an old ex-flushdecker from World War I, eight dollars a month and all the bananas you could eat. I heard that there were jobs. I asked for one—in the clothes I was standing in. They were getting ready to go, and that was under the Honduran flag."

"You went?"

"I went."

"What about your toothbrush?"

"I didn't have any."

"Extra clothes?"

"I didn't have any. We went down to the Dominican Republic and brought some bananas back. Hard, green, tasteless bananas."

"And tarantulas."

"Tarantulas, small snakes."

In Jacksonville, he hung around with seamen and with prizefighters. In an out-of-the-way place like Jacksonville, there was no regular fight card—no formal schedule of preliminary bouts.

"A bunch of us would go down to the arena, and the promoter, Jimmy Murdock, would make up five or six fights out of the ones who were there. You'd get four or five or six dollars, but it was eating money. You could eat three or four days. You could eat a week. You gave somebody a dollar for being in your corner and giving you the bandages and the tape."

He was looking for a ship, but this was before the Second World War, and ships were hard to get. He worked on a tugboat, a towboat, a homemade fishing boat, a paddle-wheel steamer called Gulf Mist. And he went on fighting. He had been on boxing teams and had fought in Golden Glove competitions during his brief days in private schools. While he rode the rails and read in libraries, he fought at night for money. He fought both "simon-pure" and semi-pro. If he won semipro, he was paid as much as ten dollars.

"Amateur, they gave you a watch and bought it back for five dollars. You could live for a week on five dollars. A hamburger steak was fifteen cents."

He fought in El Paso, Los Angeles, West Palm Beach. For five dollars, he fought in the Punch Bowl in El Paso. In Los Angeles, he had a trainer named Speedy Dado, and his manager was Joe Kelly—at Willy Orner's Main Street Gym.

"I sparred briefly with Henry Armstrong. The thing that convinced me that I wasn't going to be a fighter: I was knocked out three times in one week. I figured twice would have been enough for most folks. I carried it one more dimension."

In Brunswick, Georgia, he fought in a tent for fifty-three cents: the promoter ran off with the money, and the fighters divided what was left in the till.

In 1941, aged eighteen, he obtained his ordinary seaman's papers, and joined the oceangoing ranks of the Merchant Marine. He got a ship in Savannah. He got a ship in Charleston. He also shipped out of Port Arthur.

"I got a tanker out of there, coastwise."

He had no thought of a career at sea. Riding ships was like riding the rails.

"It was just something to do, some place to go, something that was moving."

One time, between ships, he went to West Palm Beach with a heavyweight friend who was fighting main event. The prelims were fought by servicemen picking up extra bucks, and that night all the prelim fighters' leaves were cancelled. The promoter—"Al Caroli, out of Boston"—was desperate to fill the card. Washburn and the heavyweight arrived at the National Guard Armory five minutes before the first prelim was supposed to begin. Caroli said to Washburn, "Give me a break. You fight a Mexican amateur, no big deal." Ten minutes later, the captain was on the canvas and his eyelids resembled coins.

"I got a whole twenty dollars for that," he told me. "That was the kid's last fight."

Three nights later, the Mexican amateur no-big-deal lost a ten-round decision in a Miami main event against the fourth-ranked welterweight in the world.

Looking for a ship in Charleston in January of 1943, Washburn got the John Harvey, a Liberty ship loaded with ammunition, C rations, tanks, and guns. A convoy collected at Cape Fear. Forty-five or fifty ships set out for Casablanca, soon after the Allied invasion there. One general alarm followed another, the convoy was attacked, ships went down, escorts dropped depth charges every night. He then shipped out, as a wiper, on the Howard E. Coffin, on a run to England in the winter North Atlantic. He participated in the invasion of Sicily and in the delivery of matériel to the Italian mainland. On the Moses Rogers, of the Luckenbach Steamship Company, he crossed the ocean in a convoy of a hunded and eight ships.

"In New York, the Germans were waiting for you at the sea buoy. In San Juan, they hit you at the dock. Jap submarines were inefficient. Our freighters crossed the Pacific alone. After a certain point, they zigzagged. They formed convoys only near the front. In New York, the front was at the sea buoy."

From San Francisco, in 1944, he shipped out on the Cape Henry, a C-1 diesel, operated by Lykes Brothers Steamship Company. He was an able-bodied seaman now, and sometimes sailed as bosun. He went to Saipan, where the Marines were fighting, and to Tinian, in the Marianas, and to Eniwetok Anchorage, and to Ulithi. On the John G. Tod, a Liberty ship, he did not set foot ashore for six months. He went to Kwajalein, and to Okinawa just after the American invasion. The John G. Tod stood off Okinawa for sixty-nine days. There were air raids every night, and two typhoons. Ships capsized, a couple went on reefs. The Tod was at Okinawa when the war ended.

"We paid off in San Francisco."

He had been married during the war. His wife was in Jacksonville. San Francisco was so jammed with travelling servicemen that there was no way to get out—no way to start for Florida by train or air. So he went to the union hall. Getting a ship was not difficult in 1945. Two days after arriving from the South Pacific, he was bosun of the Samuel W. Williston, and was sailing for home.

For home, but not for long. When Captain Washburn looks landward from the bridge of his ship, he will readily say, "I would rather be here for the worst that could be here than over there for the best that could be there. I've never felt comfortable or secure anywhere else. I once thought I was going to college and be a history teacher, but I have never been able to concentrate on anything else but this—not on business, family, anything. By the end of 1945, I had passed the point of no return. I was in the soup now good. Anything adverse that came up, this was my safety blanket: 'Hey, I can get a ship.' If I made plans and they went wrong, I was gone—looking for a ship."

The fact that Captain Washburn never planned to be a sailor is something he has in common with much of the Merchant Marine. He says, "Most of them aren't making a career out of this—they're just still here. A couple of guys are here only for the money. But there are a lot of us here who are here because this is where we fit in, and we don't fit in anywhere else. We seem to be out of step. The square peg in the round hole. I was out of place as a child, and now I am not looking forward to retirement. I dread it."

On the bulkhead behind his desk on the S.S. Stella Lykes is a vertical set of photographs of his wife and a daughter and the daughter's daughter and the daughter's daughter's daughter. Paul McHenry Washburn, licensed Master of United States Steam or Motor Vessels of any Gross Tons upon Oceans, is a great-grandfather. And if the day should ever come when he—like Nathaniel Bowditch, of

Salem—is the great-great-great-grandfather of someone on this ship, he intends to be here, too, as the skipper.

In 1946, after shipping out as an A.B. on the Bernuth & Lempke tanker Trimountain and the Mystic Steamship Company's Berkeley Seam, he sailed as a fireman-water tender on the United Fruit Company's Erastus Smith.

"There were jobs all over the board then. We were bringing troops home. We were feeding the world. Hey, when I was sailing, I sailed. I got off a ship and on another one the same day."

His marriage was not pacific. Not even he could say if his draw to the Merchant Marine was more of a cause or a cure. Toward the end of that year, he and his wife, Jacqueline, moved to the District of Columbia, and he became the manager of a dry-cleaning store—testing the possibilities of life on the beach. He worked there through Saturday, November 2nd. On Sunday, November 3rd, the Washington Redskins played a game of football against the Philadelphia Eagles. The Redskins are more important to Captain Washburn than any other group of people on land. They mattered no less to him then. He had developed an affectionate and protective sympathy for the Redskins after the Chicago Bears beat them 73–0 in their fourth Washington season. Washburn, who was at that game, had been following the team even before they came to Washington. He remembered them as the Boston Redskins. He remembered many of them as Duluth Eskimos. And now, on this significant Sunday in 1946, the Redskins led the Eagles

24–0 at the half. The final score was Philadelphia 28, Washington 24.

"I couldn't handle defeat like that," he says. "I can't now. I picked an argument with my wife. I remember saying, 'Listen, woman, I don't have to listen to this. I can go back to sea.' She said, 'Listen, jackass, if you go back to sea, if you come back to this house it will be so empty it will look like no one ever lived in it.' In those days, you didn't wave any red flags or throw gauntlets in front of the kid. November 7th, I was fireman and water tender on a ship out of Baltimore leaving for Poland."

"So what happened in the football game?"

"Washington sat on its lead. The Eagles' Tommy Thompson—one eye and all—hit Blackjack Ferrante in the end zone, and that was that. I still feel a little pain."

The separation led to divorce. The ship was the William S. Halstead, of Moore-McCormack Lines. She carried six thousand tons of coal and two hundred and twenty-eight cows, most of them on deck. In the Chesapeake Bay, she hit the Esso Camden, and there was a fire. Hay burned. There was a hole in the bow. She went back to Baltimore and spent seventeen days in drydock.

"Now, all of these cows had been served. Eight Quakers were along to feed and care for the cows. Three weeks to Gdansk. In the North Atlantic, half the cows had calves—a hundred and seven calves. We lost seven calves, one cow. In Gdansk, we discharged three hundred and twenty-seven head."

The Halstead went also to the east coast of South America: twenty-eight days in Rio de Janeiro, fifty-six days in Buenos Aires—the slow discharge of break-bulk cargo, the old Merchant Marine. Washburn used his free time to prepare for the Coast Guard examinations that could take him out of the fo'c'sle and make him a licensed officer. He took them and passed them in New Orleans in the summer of 1949.

"Afterward, I started looking for a ship. Jobs were tough. There weren't any ships. I couldn't get into the International Organization of Masters, Mates, and Pilots."

He may have come up the anchor chain, but the hawsepipe was solidly blocked, so he went on sailing as an able-bodied seaman. He worked on an ore carrier on the Great Lakes. He went to the west coast of South America on the Gulf Merchant.

"Then I went to New Orleans, looking for a ship. I caught the Fred Morse, a C-1, owned by Lykes Brothers Steamship Company."

A sailor always remains something of a freelance, but this was the beginning of a relationship that only age would end. The company derived from the Spanish-American Sealift, and Washburn would be with it so long that people would someday imagine that he did, too. The seven founding Lykes brothers were from Hillsborough County, Florida. Since early in this century, the company has made its headquarters in New Orleans. Among major American shipping companies, it seems to be competing with Sea-Land and

American President Lines for that special form of venerability that is reserved for the last of anything. The last Mohican. The last passenger pigeon. Third mate, second mate, chief mate—Washburn kept taking his Coast Guard exams between voyages all over the earth on various Lykes Brothers ships. He first sailed as master on Lykes Brothers' Anadarko Victory. He has been the skipper of—among many other ships—the Sylvia Lykes, the Sue Lykes, the Charlotte Lykes ("She was a South and East African ship"), the Sheldon Lykes, the Jean Lykes, the Mallory Lykes, the Genevieve Lykes. In 1979, he took the Genevieve with a load of cotton to Tsingtao, in the Yellow Sea. A month earlier, the Letitia Lykes, under another master, had called at Shanghai. In thirty years, these were the first two American merchant ships to load for China. After Washburn secured the Genevieve, forty officials climbed the gangway to clear the ship, including naval architects. To the dockside came a very long line of children, walking two by two and holding hands. Thousands of people came to see the ship.

Across all the years, Washburn kept in touch with his former wife. He followed news of her as she remarried, as she gave birth to children, and, ultimately, as she suffered the dissolution of her second marriage as well. If she needed support in any form, he was always there to help. In 1976, between runs to South and East Africa as master of the Sheldon Lykes, he asked her to marry him. She decided that she could deal with him even if the Redskins lost. They live in a multilevel condominium behind the third green at the Baymeadows Golf & Country Club, in Jacksonville, where he has an American flag flying from their bedroom balcony, as if it were the fantail of a ship.

Andy thinks that I should visit him there, visit him and others in their homes, so that I can see merchant mariners in their contrasting lives: see the undisputed master of any gross tons upon oceans in contexts where in all likelihood he is the undisputed master of nothing. Washburn tees up at Baymeadows, a quiet place under pines and palms. Wearing an electric-blue shirt, red pants, and white shoes, he is himself an American flag. According to his closest friend, a New Orleans businessman named Edward Lee, Washburn has spent twenty thousand dollars on golf lessons and golf equipment. His irons are Hogan Radials. He addresses his ball with a custom-made, frequency-balanced, titanium-boron-graphite driver. He waves it over the ball as if he were rubbing a lamp.

I remember asking him, on the ship, what he does with his long vacations, which he has to take in order to share his job.

"If the whole truth is known, most of the eighty-five days I am sitting around waiting to go back to work," he said. "I'm impatient if it's eighty-five days. If I have to take four or five months off, I go berserk. I play golf incessantly. I'm out there thrashing away, screaming, cursing, throwing clubs, making a spectacle of myself. They don't call me Captain Angry for nothing. Which is my nickname in the club I belong to. I hate golf. I hate it with a passion. I hate it because I can't do it better. It's a major defeat."

And now, at Baymeadows, seconds before his first tee shot, he mutters, "There is nothing I love as much as I hate this game."

According to Edward Lee, Washburn has long since composed the inscription he wants on his tombstone:

I'D RATHER BE HERE
THAN PLAYING GOLF

He swings. He hits the ball two hundred yards up the middle. His second shot goes another two hundred yards up the middle. He is on the green in three, very nearly sinks a thirty-foot putt, and is down in par five.

With three companions, he is playing skins no carry-over, which means, among other things, that only a clear winner wins a hole. He is the clear winner of seventy-five cents. The foursome includes Craig Van Horn, who is in charge of sales for Weyerhaeuser in Florida and, as we go along, converses by telephone from his golf cart with salesmen all over the state.

Washburn describes the second at Baymeadows as "the most honest but difficult No. 2 hole in the city." When the hole, in its probity, puts him into a sand trap, he says, "They don't call me the Desert Fox for nothing. The kid could always get out of the sand." The Desert Fox raises a cloud of sediment, but the kid remains in the sand.

On the fifth hole, his ball comes to rest between two trees that stand closer than bollards. "Greed, avarice," he mumbles, referring to the risk inherent in the shot that put him in the trees. Trying to get out, he lands in sand. He pars the seventh. On the tenth, as his titanium tee shot turns left like a model airplane on a tether, he says, "The kid can always hook 'em." On the fifteenth, his golf cart is rear-ended. ("You sail defensively. . . . Hey, the *only* way I'm going to get hit is in the stern.")

Peewee, in Savannah, takes me down Victory Drive, calling it "the longest palm drive in the world," showing off his home town. "They been here hundreds of years," he says of the columnar trees. "Way before I was born." In and out among horses and buggies he weaves through Johnson Square. Peewee's own buggy, his Lincoln Town Car in dark cabernet clear-coat, is a rubber-borne cabin cruiser with cruise control and a burglar alarm. He paid twenty-six thousand for it new. His wife, Ethel Kennedy, has it much of the year, after taking him to Charleston to put him on his ship. When I ask her how long a trip that is, she says, "If I'm nice, two hours."

"What if you're not nice?"

"An hour and a half."

Ethel describes Peewee's absence as "a lonesome missing piece." Years ago, he used to ship out of Savannah, on United States Lines vessels to North Europe. A cadre of their seven children would go with her when she took him to the waterfront, and one time a grandnephew went along and kept saying, "Put me in his seabag, put me in his seabag." Ethel, recalling this, says, "He looked like his heart would drop out of his body." The kids waved at the ship as it went down the Savannah River. Peewee, on deck, waved back. He would be gone fifty days.

They live in a one-story house painted dusty gold on a street that is shaded with sycamores. There are two heavily bearing pecans in their yard, near a brick barbecue so large that it could be the standing remains of a house that burned down. Ethel has landscaped their corner lot, with no help from Peewee. She will not let him mow the lawn, regarding him as incompetent. He sits in the house, relaxing for three months, with a cigar in his shirt pocket—the provider. His daughters Diane and Louvenia come in and hit him for fifty cents so they can go up the street for sodas. Diane is thirty-four and Louvenia is thirty-three. On the piano, in the dining room, is a ship in a bottle. Over the tropical plants on the glassed-in porch turns a slow paddle fan. The rest of the house is air-conditioned. In, among other things, ceramic objects that Ethel makes, there is ample evidence in every room of the presence of religion. A masked gunman not long ago came close to destroying this domestic scene. He came off the street, demanded money, and shot Ethel in the neck and the collarbone. In the hospital, she watched the doctor for a while and said, "Am I fixin' to die?" He said no, and she believed him. She had been wearing a thick gold chain. The bullet severed it, but the chain saved her.

Married to Peewee nearly forty years, Ethel has a concise and summary view of the Merchant Marine. She says, "It was the chance to give us a good living."

Whatever Peewee may be thinking when he crosses the equator, he concurs. "We don't owe nobody," he explains. "We got it made."

David Carter, the deck and engine mechanic, drives north to Charleston from his home in Jacksonville in a Dodge van that is more than ten years old and shows a hundred thousand miles. But he, too, may have it made. When he is not on the ocean, he buys and refurbishes houses, in one of which he lives, with his wife, Peggy, a hospital record keeper, and their two sons. In the escalating process of buying and selling property, he has acquired six acres of pondfront and canalfront land under laurel oaks and cypress in a lovely section of Jacksonville that attracts the lust of yuppies. The zoning is quarter-acre. Quarter-acre lots in the area are selling for sixty thousand dollars. Twenty-four times sixty thousand is one million four hundred and forty thousand. He will not realize that much, but less will do.

Meanwhile, the Carters live in Neptune Beach, some blocks from the water, in a small place with six banana trees and a neighbor who poured paint thinner on their garden plants. David says dreamily, as he barbecues a chicken, "I was tempted to skin his dog and hang it to his front door." One of the schools David taught in is around the corner. He is a graduate of Tulane and taught for ten years—math and social studies as well as Spanish—before he discovered that he could make four times as much painting valve wheels at sea as he could teaching children on land. His great-uncles were Norwegian merchant seamen. His mother has a family tree that is littered with phrases like "buried at sea," "died at sea," "lost at sea." At home, as on the ocean, he studies engineering, preparing himself to come up the hawsepipe. "In the engine room, the four-to-eight watch is usually everybody's last choice," he remarks. "You get stuck with a lot of maneuvering. You are always arriving or leaving port on the four-to-eight. But when I get a ship I ask for that watch. The second is always pumping oil, testing water, et cetera, leaving the demac to do many things a licensed engineer would ordinarily do. You learn more."

In the captain's home, across town, the numerous religious calendars are outnumbered by the golfing trophies he has won in the pro-am tournaments of the Fellowship of Christian Athletes. Some of the condos in his neighborhood stand like ships in sculpted bayous. Outside the Washburns' sliding doors is terra firma. Routinely, a neighbor's cat comes into the house and sits beside the captain while he eats. The morsels he slips to the neighbor's cat are by human standards attractive. Just outside is a small ornamental tree. Squirrels linger beneath it, because they, too, are fed by the captain. Suddenly, the cat shoots out from under the table and mortally wounds a squirrel. Captain Washburn himself is almost mortally stricken. The goodness of his heart has caused the death of a squirrel. Repeatedly, he leaves his bacon, his eggs and grits, and goes out to observe the squirrel, barely clinging, swaying, on a branch of the ornamental tree. As the cat is fully aware, the captain's benevolent guilt does not end there. He attracts more birds than St. Francis, because he feeds them, too.

("Tell him to be my guest, then, if the horses prefer wood. Tell him I'm sorry I don't have barley or oats.")

In the captain's car, we go for an evening drive with Jackie, his wife, and Tinker, his visiting daughter. I have asked to see the place where Harriet Beecher Stowe grew oranges. Captain Washburn, at the wheel, requires the assistance of a mate. Jackie guides him toward Mandarin, every turn. To his dismay, she becomes absorbed in some talk about oranges with me. He says, "Jack, if you don't pay attention to where we're going, we're lost, because half of us are always lost." He is confessing the artless truth: ashore, he has no sense of reckoning, dead or alive. On the road, he has no idea where he is going. By his own description, he gets hopelessly lost in his own driveway. Looking for an interstate highway, he ignores the numbered shields. He goes right past the huge green signs. In the confusion of the moment, he refers to a nearby two-door car as a two-car door.

I think of him in the Panama Canal. Given his distaste for terrestrial navigation, you might imagine that he would be only too happy to turn things over to professional pilots for a fifty-mile trip through a jungle. But this was a ship, not a Chevrolet. He would not be unconfident as he moved south and east to get to the Pacific. From lock to lock, from sea buoy to sea buoy, he was right there fussing all the way across the continent. He wore his dress blues with shoulder boards, which tended to suggest that he was in charge, but he was not. The pilots were in complete command. Most of them were still being provided by the United States Merchant Marine. Thaddeus Kowal, of New Orleans, for example, was a former chief mate of Sea-Land vessels and had been a Panama Canal pilot for sixteen years. As he tucked the ship into Lower Gatun Lock, I thought, New Orleans? Kowal? Saul, Sheldon, Stewart, Stephen, Stanley Kowal? I asked him if a little something might be missing in his name.

No, he said. He was a Panama Canal pilot, not a character in a play. "*Kowal* means 'blacksmith,' " he went on. "*Ski* means 'son of.' My father used to drink it up, and say, 'We *are* the blacksmith.' " Balder than a monk—in cowboy boots, silver-rimmed glasses, a sky-blue sateen guayabera—Kowal was sixty-two.

"Left twenty," he said.

"Left twenty," said the helmsman.

"Midships."

"Midships."

"Dead slow ahead."

Kowal killed a mosquito. Captain Washburn killed a mosquito. Captain Washburn sprayed himself. He had a can of Off marked "BRIDGE." To carry a can of insect repellent on the bridge of his ship was no less repellent to him than it was to the insects. In half a century of trips through the canal, he had only in recent times encountered his first mosquito. After so many chemically antiseptic, pesticidally bugless American years, to Captain Washburn the mosquito's sting was deeper than the length of one proboscis.

"Port twenty," said the pilot.

"Left twenty," said the helmsman.

"Hard left," said the pilot.

"Hard left," said the helmsman.

"Hard left," said Captain Washburn.

After the quartermaster, at the wheel, repeated the pilot's commands, the captain, as if in need to be a part of things, sometimes repeated them, too. The pilots used "left" and "right" to conform to Coast Guard rules for helm commands on American ships. Occasionally, they forgot themselves and threw in a "port" or a "starboard," the helm commands used on the ships of the rest of the world. Signs hang in wheelhouses to remind officers and sailors to say "left" and "right" when giving and acknowledging helm commands, for "port" and "starboard" are used throughout the ship for every other purpose. American sailors on sweetwater ships (on the Great Lakes) say "left" and "right" wherever they are—and "floor," "wall," and "kitchen"—but not on ships of any gross tons upon oceans.

One of our pilots was Jonas Thorsteinsson, a fountain of sea stories and the author of the basic Icelandic text on celestial navigation. He is a naturalized American citizen, and, like all the other canal pilots, has four weeks of vacation for every six weeks he works. His home and family are in Pensacola. As skipper of a research vessel in the North Pacific, he once dropped an anchor that took nearly half an hour to reach bottom. He said all these things as he moved the Stella Lykes from lock to lock, easily juggling his stories with his commands to the helmsman. He told me about the Icelandic child Snorri Thorfinsson, who was born on an island in the Delaware River, quite near the site of Philadelphia, in June, 1002.

"Hard right."

"Hard right."

"Slow astern."

The baby's father was Thorfinnur Karlsefni, Jonas said. The baby's mother was Gudridur Thorbjarnsdottir. Jonas had read Thorfinnur's logs at the National Library in Reykjavik. After three years, Thorfinnur and family had left Philadelphia under pressure from unfriendly natives. The family returned to Iceland. In 1021, Pope Benedict VIII learned of these adventures and invited Thorfinnur to Rome. Thorfinnur was sick and could not travel, but Gudridur went to the Vatican. She told the Pope about the birth of her child and her life on the island in—as it was then called—the Lenape River. Such stories were common in eleventh-century Iceland, Jonas said. In 1491, or earlier, Columbus went to Iceland to be briefed.

Southbound and northbound, we went through the canal with an aggregate of sixty-six ships. Only two others were flying the American flag. Southbound, in the entire day, we were the only vessel of the United States Merchant Marine. We crossed Gatun Lake under a full moon that shuffled light through scattered low dark clouds. The lake is artificial, but now that it is there a nature conservancy would want to preserve it. The channel picked its way through countless jungled islands. The fixed green stars were range lights, the blinking green stars were buoys. At night, the jungle cools, the cool air flows to the warm canal and makes a strip of fog.

Northbound, we tied up in fog in the locks of Pedro Miguel. A Panama Railroad train, old and decrepit, went by with its windows open. The air-conditioning had broken down in the railroad's newer cars, the captain said. The old ones were in use "so that the people inside can at least open the windows." He said the tracks were loose. He said that Gatun Lake was silting in. "Eventually, there won't be a Panama Canal," he continued. "Anywhere in the world, if you fool with Mother Nature she's going to get you. This is not a political statement. It is just a fact." He slapped his arm. "We're back to the yellow-fever days," he said. "Back to the jungle. There won't be any streets. There won't be anything. It will be like North Africa when the Arabs took over—all those beautiful condominiums with goats in them. I wish you could have seen this twenty-five years ago, when we ruled the ocean, when we were the elite." It had all been neat and trig and spruce. It had been a clean swath across the tropics. Now the concrete was becoming rubbled. Steel drums and other detritus were strewn about. In the Gatun locks, a pilot said, "See that dirt laying there where they're working on the mule tracks? Come back ten years from now and that'll still be there."

Another pilot said, "Anyone who thinks the Panamanians can run this canal is a dreamer. The Japanese will run it. The Japanese bank is the only one that didn't close when others did."

Captain Washburn said, "We can get along without this canal. Japan and Russia can't."

Pairs of men in rowboats tied lines from the ship to lines from locomotive mules. The mules helped to pull the ship through. The mules whistled like trains. Panamanian canal seamen in hard hats worked the fantail. One kept saying, "Sex book?" Another flashed a packet of white powder in the palm of his hand.

The Miraflores locks had broken down. One of the pairs of gates that meet in the middle was not meeting in the middle. The pilot said, "The gates weigh seven hundred and forty-five tons but are so perfectly balanced they can be turned by hand." They were indeed being turned by hand. It was the only way to close the lock. The captain rolled his eyes and shrugged. He said, "Another day in the life of Walter Mitty. Heavens to Murgatroyd, we're stuck in the lock."

In Balboa, a crippled dying fish went round and round in circles between the ship and the dock, swimming beside the corpse of a thick-bodied snake. The tropical fresh water was stiff with plastic flotsam. Victor Belmosa said, "You could drink the water in years gone by. The dock here you could eat off of in years gone by." These remarks notwithstanding, Victor was fishing, on the offshore side—Victor, with his zirconia ring in his left ear, his tattoos on both arms, his goatee, dropping a hand line for red snapper. Victor had also caught yellowtails, eels, catfish, and corvina there, off the side of the ship in Balboa. More than a third of the sailors fish off the ship. To improve their luck, they hang floodlights over the side. "There's forty-five feet of water here," Victor said. "Sometimes we have seventy fish on deck here." Duke Labaczewski had fished in the locks themselves. He said, "Saltwater fish go with the ship from lock to lock, you can see them." In the open sea, when the ship slows down, Duke has caught bonito and dolphin and barracuda, and Spanish mackerel four feet long. If barracuda come into Balboa, he said, their mouths will become green and their flesh poisonous. From an old Cuban fisherman Duke learned years ago to cut a hole in the side of a barracuda and insert a silver coin. If the coin turns black, the fish is no good. If the coin continues to shine, cure the barracuda with salt and call it bacalao. In the Guayas River, Duke has caught what he describes as "big big catfish with heads like basketballs." David Carter, on another ship, once fished in the ocean using parachute shrouds for a line. He caught "huge fish" and reeled them in with the ship's winch. He has no idea what they were.

Washburn in the Caribbean, this man who could not find his way around a traffic circle, had to dodge—outwit and outmaneuver—a tropical storm. The National Hurricane Center was issuing advisories. The route he had planned would often be close to islands, banks, and shoals: Cayos del Este Sudeste, Isla de Providencia, Roncador Bank, Quita Sueño Bank, the Northwest Rocks of Serraña Bank—a seascape blooming with wrecks. At first, the water was flat calm. The Caribbean air, as usual, was thicker than the jungle air of Panama, heavy as a rubber blanket. (I have never understood why anyone would pay for it.) While

Tropical Depression No. 7 was dumping seven inches of rain on Puerto Rico in as many hours, Washburn took as constant its course (285) and speed (fifteen knots) and stepped off on a chart its future positions. The predicted winds were "sixty-five miles an hour and developing." The term "developing" included but was not limited to "explosive deepening."

"When these things decide to develop into something bigger, it's almost instantaneous," Washburn said. "You can be five hundred miles away from it, and think you're safe, and suddenly it reaches out. If we go to Yucatan, we and the storm will arrive at Cape San Ann Tone at exactly the same time. In this game, it's the ties that hurt. The dead heats. We're going under that sucker and east."

He headed straight for the storm in order to be where it had been. And he avoided rushing to confined waters. After forty-eight hours or so, he reached the track of the storm, and stood on the bridge looking out on the lazy waves of a sunlit Caribbean. "On a day like this," he said, "even the In God We Trust could have made it."

Fragments of the future and fragments of the past—all that was a thousand leagues away as we sailed north to Lima and returned to Guayaquil.

On the dock in Callao, the seaport of Lima, we left a container said to contain thirty thousand pounds of chewing-gum base. The manifest advised the mate, "Please stow away from the boilers." We left a container said to contain fifteen thousand pounds of "hot leftovers," which were otherwise unexplained. We left twelve thousand pounds of "synthetic organic pigments." We left sixteen containers said to contain five hundred thousand pounds of yarn. We left forty-seven hundred bags of cellulose-acetate flakes. We left raw tobacco, processed fats, malic acid, industrial hoists. We left three tons of fluorescent tubes, twenty tons of float glass, and thirty-three tons of steel angles. We left two graders, a bulldozer, and a hundred and ten bags of common clay. We left twenty tons of chicken vitamins. We left twenty-five hundred tons of sardines to be collected by Japanese ships.

Approaching Callao, Andy saw, for the first time northbound, the handle of the Big Dipper. From the northern rim of the earth it protruded like the handle of a plow. Closer to shore was an apparently permanent mist, too thin to be fog, too thick to be haze, and hanging so heavy it was almost rain. On the three-centimetre radar, the numerous ships at anchor looked like dotted clouds. Most were Russian; some were former Dutch, Italian, and British warships, long ago sold to Peru. Captain Washburn said, "If they move, they are towed." Captain Washburn, in dress blues, had appeared on the bridge in the morning not long after four.

The Callao pilot, a compact man of middle age named Jorge Bustamante, guided the ship through the narrow aperture of the Callao breakwater speaking English to the quartermaster and Spanish to the tugs, and quoting Peruvian proverbs. "Have a son, plant a tree, write a book," he said. And all in the space of ten seconds he said, "Stop her. A little push ahead. *Muy despacio.* Stop her. Another push, Captain. Dead slow ahead. *Poco más fuerte.* Stop her."

"Roger," said Washburn.

"All to the right," said Bustamante.

"Hard right," said Washburn.

Bustamante told us that he would have risen to high places in the Peruvian Navy but had been prevented from doing so because he was honest. He also said, "Whenever I board an American ship, I can smell America."

I asked what the smell was like.

He said, "Clean."

It could be said, though, that almost anything entering that milieu would seem clean. A person could confide to a notebook:

> Callao is a filthy, ill-built, small seaport. . . . The city of Lima is now in a wretched state of decay: the streets are nearly unpaved; and heaps of filth are piled up in all directions.

As Darwin did in 1835. The picture he painted has not faded or changed. The midden reeks in the medians of roads.

> The black gallinazos, tame as poultry, pick up bits of carrion. The houses have generally an upper story, built, on account of the earthquakes, of plastered woodwork; but some of the old ones, which are now used by several families, are immensely large, and would rival in suites of apartments the most magnificent in any place. Lima, the City of the Kings, must formerly have been a splendid town.

Darwin could publish that now. He could be working as a stringer. His dispatches could be filed to *The New York Times*.

> No State in South America, since the declaration of independence, has suffered more from anarchy than

> Peru. At the time of our visit, there were four chiefs in arms contending for supremacy in the government: if one succeeded in becoming for a time very powerful, the others coalesced against him.

> A dull heavy bank of clouds constantly hung over the land. . . . It is almost become a proverb, that rain never falls in the lower part of Peru. Yet this can hardly be considered correct; for during almost every day of our visit there was a thick drizzling mist, which was sufficient to make the streets muddy and one's clothes damp: this the people are pleased to call Peruvian dew.

Off the dock there we picked up four hundred and twenty-two thousand pounds of coffee and a hundred thousand pounds of shrimp. We picked up four containers said to contain five thousand bags of "chilled" lead shot. We picked up zinc oxide and alpaca blankets. We picked up cotton, tuna, tungsten, and a ton of terry-cloth towels. We picked up a 1942 Chevrolet convertible destined to fetch a large price in the rich marketplace of antique cars. Under a New York gavel you could sell a Latin American traffic jam for ten million dollars.

And now it is 5:49 A.M., August 18th, and Vernon McLaughlin turns the helm over to Calvin King, saying, "Zero-three-nine. Automatic. All is well, and the pirates are waiting for us." Three degrees south of the equator, we are crossing the Gulf of Guayaquil. For the second time, we approach the Guayas. The sea is flat. The temperature is cool (in the sixties). In the weeks since we were here before, the pirate talk has never really stopped, but now, as we prepare once more to go upstream, the talk intensifies. "This place is becoming a God-damned war zone," Mac says. "When you board a ship that is docking, how much more brazen can you get? That is real defiance."

"We didn't sign anything saying that we would defend this ship with our lives," Andy remarks.

In the past couple of months in Guayaquil, pirates have attacked the Allison Lykes once, the Mallory Lykes once, and the Stella Lykes three times. Late one evening, some of Stella's crew saw pirates boarding a vessel berthed a cable length away. The port authorities were notified. Meanwhile, the spectators watched goods from containers being lowered into small boats from the stern of the other ship. They witnessed the arrival of police, who had a look around and left. The pirates resumed work. Thirteen boatloads went to the mangrove swamps.

One attack occurred at noon. Obviously, the pirates have no fear of confrontation. "They know our routines," the captain remarks. "They know if we're eating supper. They know if we're heaving up the anchor. They know where every man on the ship is. They have free run of the harbor. They've come aboard with manifests. They go around looking for the containers with the TVs, the containers with the computers. Piracy is a way of life here. It has been for four hundred years. We've had 'em steal the flag halyards, the mooring lines. Any kind of metal. The sounding caps out of the deck. The deck telephones. Mooring lines are chained down and locked. They can cut those chains like they're paper. What can we do? We'll have roving patrols, crew members on the stern with walkie-talkies, searchlights."

J. Peter Fritz, the chief mate, says, "They carry firearms. They have bolt cutters. They know their way around the ship in darkness. They know our lashing gear. They know our docking procedures. They must have walkie-talkies. They must have people with spyglasses."

A couple of trips ago, in Guayaquil, an A.B. named Bill Haisten went aft at dawn to run up the flag and cut some lights. When he didn't return, Luke Midgett sent Calvin and Peewee to investigate. They found Haisten tied to a king post. Seven pirates had come over the stern and surprised him. In their needle boat, they had come up the river under the stern of the ship before the day's first light. They were armed mainly with knives. One of them held a hacksaw blade at Haisten's throat while others tied him up. A sailor named Ron Just, who was taking "a morning stroll," happened to pick the wrong moment to stroll across the stern. They tied him to the lashing rods of a container. A pirate pointed at the men's watches and said, "Give me." When Just showed signs of not cooperating, the pirate threatened to cut off Just's arm with a hacksaw. Haisten and Just surrendered the watches. The pirate looked at Haisten's watch and gave it back.

Breaking into four containers, the pirates stole a load of yard goods. Then they went over the side and away in their boat. "But, hey," the captain says. "Hey! They take whole containers in New York, in Boston. They don't board from private boats. You're safe until the longshoremen and the labor gangs come aboard. They think it's part of their pay. No one outsteals the Boston longshoremen. They wouldn't *have* that. Ever since man put two logs together and made a raft, people stole from it. During the war, when I was an able seaman somewhere in North Africa I watched two Arabs work two hours to take a mattress through a porthole. They got a corner of it up there—they twisted and pulled and they twisted and pulled, and they finally got that whole mattress through the porthole. Then the chief mate took it away from them. But, hey! Piracy is a different ballgame. Sooner or later, they start killing people."

Off Singapore, when merchant ships make the slow tight move between Raffles Lighthouse and Buffalo Rock they might as well be passing through a pirate tollhouse. It is most especially that part of the Strait of Malacca which is in a category with the approaches to Lagos, with various ports in the Bight of Benin, with Guayaquil. After pirate attacks in the Malacca Strait, it has been reported that the pirates were wearing uniforms. They use gunboats. They have sprayed merchant ships with automatic weapons.

To throw a grappling hook over a stern rail and climb a line to board a ship requires conditioned strength. The pirates have that kind of strength. Our quinquagenarian and sexagenarian crewmen—so many of whom appear to be in their third trimester—are no match for such invaders. The day may come when merchant ships are beribboned with concertina wire, railed with chain-link fencing.

In Charleston, Captain Ron Crook told me that he had once lain at anchor off the delta of the Ganges for two weeks as he waited to transfer cargo to a German ship. Every night, in heavy rain, pirates came down the river in black mahogany boats. These were oar-powered boats, each holding ten or fifteen pirates. Crook blew his whistle and shouted commands—including "Repel boarders!"—while the crew shot water into the boats from high-pressure hoses. The pirates had bamboo poles with hooks on the end. They climbed them to the deck. The crew fought the boarders with axe handles, broom handles, and three-cell flashlights. At last, the Germans arrived. They brought two hundred Indians of both sexes and all ages to unload the ship by hand, to lighten it enough to go up the shallow Ganges to Calcutta. The Indians camped on Crook's deck, where they built fires and made curries. Crook is a great-great-great-nephew of Brigadier General George Crook, commander of the Department of the Platte, who was one of the most celebrated soldiers of the Old West, and who stood out in his time for the integrity with which he dealt with Indians.

In 1974, when Ron Crook was third mate on the Mormacscan, armed pirates boarded her in Brazilian waters, went directly to a container said to contain two hundred thousand dollars' worth of Kodak film, offloaded all the film, and sped away in a small, fast boat.

Captain Washburn says, "Hey, Cartagena it happens. Buenaventura. In Buenaventura, a while back, they boarded ships while they were under way. It took the United Nations to stop it. In Buenaventura, while the Mason Lykes was steaming around the sea buoy—waiting for daylight *because* of piracy—a pirate grappled the rail, came aboard with a gun, held up the third mate, took his wallet and watch, and disappeared. But, hey, a couple of guys disguised as longshoremen went on a Waterman ship in Barbour's Cut, Houston, Texas, and walked right into the captain's office, made him open the safe, took the money, and shot him dead. Pretty soon—down here on the west coast of South America—it's going to get violent. Right now you'll see armed guards. That's fairly new. Pretty soon these pirates will start shooting back if they get shot at."

In Callao, after a new pilot ladder worth five thousand dollars went over the side and into a waiting boat, Louis Smothers said, "What goes around comes back." In case anyone misunderstood him, he explained that we, as a nation, "stole people's lands and destroyed their minds," and are now getting what we deserve. Smothers, an A.B. on the twelve-to-four, was the assistant pastor of a church in York, Pennsylvania, before he moved to Jacksonville. There he has become an intraurban itinerant preacher, preaching every Sunday in a different church when he is home from the sea. He has been shipping out with the Merchant Marine for twenty-seven years. Before that, he was in theological seminary, and before that he spent many years in the army. He once owned what he describes as "the largest black detective agency in the state of Maryland." He often wears shorts. They reveal the legs of a football player. On his dark-blue baseball cap are the words "QUEEN MARY," across the brow in gold. "The Peruvians steal a line or a ladder or something from a container," he went on. "In New York, they steal your Mercedes and put it *in* a container, and six days later it's in Panama."

On every deck of the Stella Lykes, signs are hung on the doors that connect the interior of the house to the open outside spaces:

THIS DOOR TO BE KEPT CLOSED AND
DOGGED IN ALL FOREIGN PORTS

The doors are dogged to keep out more than pirates. Captain Washburn, who happens to be in his quarters now, lathering up for his morning shave and listening to his tape of "Heartaches," says, "This coast is not only the drug-producing capital of the world; it is also the stowaway-producing capital of the world. Why the ships here don't have more of each is a mystery. We fight it and fight it and fight it. We try our best to hold it to a minimum." Some years ago, the word "contraband" referred, generally, to souvenirs illegally transported by crewmen, he went on. "When you are talking about contraband now, you are talking about narcotics—hashish, marijuana, cocaine, heroin. That stuff is doubly hard to find. Usually it's in very small packages. They can hide it in a light fixture or a shoe."

As for stowaways, Washburn has found very few of them on ships of which he has been master—and that is most fortunate, he adds, because stowaways are a major nuisance. If they turn up on your ship, you pay a fine. You do a great deal of paperwork. You post a sizable bond. You don't get it back if they escape. When they go off the ship, you have to hire guards to guard them. You have to see that they are put on the right plane. "If you bring in twenty stowaways, you're looking at a couple of hundred thousand dollars. You're looking at big bucks."

One does not have to be a former hobo to understand that the seriousness of the stowaway problem is not in a category with the drug traffic. I cannot help wondering, though, what this son of the side-door sleeping cars, this former rider of the rails, would do with stowaways if he found them on his ship.

I ask him, and he says, "I'd take the handcuffs and the leg irons and lock them up."

On a dock in Colombia during the previous voyage, Ron Peterson, the third mate, was about to inspect a container when a Colombian longshoreman rushed up and put a Lykes Brothers seal on it. This was to be the last container loaded on the ship, and Peterson knew that it was said to contain nothing and therefore did not require a seal. He described the scene to the chief mate, who came down the gangway, broke the seal, and looked in. Nine faces looked out.

Ecuadorian and Colombian longshoremen loading American ships used to build huts deep in the holds and bury stowaways in mountains of coffee. Some ships have diverted steam lines into cargo compartments and used a steam smothering system to flush out possible stowaways. Some have used whistles at deafening frequencies. After Delta Lines did that, Colombia complained to the United

Nations. Not long ago, the Sheldon Lykes arrived in Mobile, Alabama, with twenty-one Colombian stowaways aboard. A West German ship turned up in Jacksonville with four Ethiopians. The youngest was twelve, the oldest fifteen. Heading south, the crew of the Allison Lykes found a stowaway who had got on in New York.

At the end of another recent voyage, the Allison arrived in Port Newark carrying a container said to contain chocolate and addressed to a warehouse in Long Island. The United States Customs Service drilled into the chocolate and found a filling of cocaine. They resealed the container. It was offloaded, set on a tractor trailer, and driven away. Customs agents followed. At the Long Island warehouse, they arrested the recipients of the chocolate, who were members of the Medellín Cartel. Inside the chocolate was four hundred and eighty million dollars' worth of cocaine —the largest single shipment of cocaine ever seized in a United States port north of Florida.

"They just try to catch what they can," Washburn comments. "They figure they stop less than ten per cent of it." When the Customs people appeared in Newark with fifteen dogs and unloaded seventy of Stella's containers right there on the dock, they found nothing. Nevertheless, they charged the people to whom the containers were addressed seventy-five dollars per container. When they do discover drugs, they not only will fine the shipping company but will confiscate whole ships. They fined Evergreen, of the Taiwan flag, fifty-nine and a half million dollars after eleven thousand pounds of marijuana turned up in New Orleans.

"It's our problem, but there's nothing we can do about it," Washburn continues. "The letter of the law is that a ship is responsible for everything it brings in. But we're not there when the containers are packed. When they deliver a container down here, you certainly don't make them take the cargo out of it. They've now got containers that are built to smuggle. They've got a double wall. You couldn't detect it if you were in there. We pick up containers and we load them, and there's absolutely no way we can check the contents. We've got a piece of paper that says what's in there. 'Said to contain'—that's all we've got. Half of these drugs are smuggled in in household articles—like they've got refrigerators and dryers just full of them, and overstuffed furniture. But the real kingpins are much more sophisticated than that. It's a computerized business today. It's not piecemeal or haphazard. Where they've got three or four hundred million dollars' worth coming in, the cartel may have spent two years setting that one delivery up. They even start when they're refining it. They say, 'O.K., we're refining this amount. It's eventually going to go to New York in *this* type of container.' They'll even *build* a container for that special shipment. These clever Colombians—they trap wild dogs and keep them penned up. They use the urine of the wild dogs to smear on the packages of cocaine that they're sending in to the United States. These domestic dogs that we're using smell that wild-dog urine and they're afraid, and they don't go near that stuff. There'll be a day that these dogs will be useless to us and we'll be using pigs. They find something. We combat it. They find something else. The drug lords threaten everyone. Oh, they're tough. They've caught American drug enforcers, and they've killed more than one, and they didn't kill 'em quick, either. It took some of them two or three days to die. Just like the old days, you know—two or three days and just begging for death. These Colombians don't just kill a person. They'll kill a guy's mother and father, his wife, his children. They kill the whole family. There's a viciousness about these present drug dealers that the old Mafia—the old underworld—never had. The old underworld treated each other bad enough, but they weren't vicious to the general populace, ever. It was bad for business. They thought nothing of shooting or blowing up their adversary, but they never thought about hitting a guy's women and children. It wasn't their nature. But, man, these drug lords—they'll terrorize a whole community to have their way. They had one prosecutor in Colombia that the drug lords told him they were going to kill him and they told him there was nowhere he could hide. They told him, 'Between the North Pole and the South Pole there is nowhere you can go that we won't find you. There's no such place.' I think it was Sofia, Bulgaria, they caught up with him and killed him. That's what an honest official is up against. In Ecuador, my gosh, they're killing a prosecutor or a judge every day in the week."

On one of Stella's voyages, under another captain, a Colombian brought to the ship a twenty-kilogram carton labeled as coffee. He said it was for the bosun, and he departed. Crew members routinely buy Colombian coffee, but not the brand mentioned on the carton. The bosun said he had purchased none. Lock it up, said the captain. After the ship sailed, he ordered an inspection. According to Peewee, who was working that voyage, the box contained well over a million dollars' worth of uncut crack—twelve tightly wrapped packets of white powder, at any rate, each weighing more than three and a half pounds. The captain told the mate to break open the packets and pour the contents into the ocean. "That saved a lot of paperwork," Peewee said as he finished telling the story. "A lot of paperwork and a lot of jive." The deliveryman had evidently erred. Not long before he reached the dock, another ship had sailed for the United States.

Some years ago, after a sailor just off the Joseph Lykes was found with two million dollars' worth of cocaine, Lykes Brothers was fined two hundred thousand dollars. Washburn believes that American sailors do very little smuggling anymore. Among other things, they have come to know that people who sell drugs to Americans are likely to go straight to the American Embassy and report the transaction in order to claim a finder's fee. The United States pays finder's fees of up to fifty thousand dollars.

Washburn likes to tell a story about an old Lykes Brothers stick ship that "brought a couple and their camper-type van from the Gulf down to either Colombia or Ecuador on this run, and put them off." He continues, "What these people were going to do was tour South America, and then they were going to come back on this same ship to the United States. They left the ship in either Guayaquil or Buenaventura—I forget which. Weeks later, the couple came aboard, with their ticket and everything, and the ship was loading their camper. The chief mate happened to notice that the ship's cargo gear—those single-stick booms—could hardly pick that camper up. They got it aboard, but just barely. And he became suspicious, and they searched that camper, and there was three tons of cocaine in a special-built floor in the bottom of the camper. It was not in there haphazard. It was almost like that camper had been rebuilt. Three tons of cocaine is worth about a hundred and eighty million dollars."

Washburn stares for a while into the passing mangroves, the ragged edge of the olive river. Then he says, "The basis of the problem is the American appetite for this stuff. I can put everybody else down, but *we're the customers*. I'm sittin' here puttin' Colombia, Bolivia, and Ecuador down, and *we're* the customers. It's *our* ferocious appetite. It's an illness. And if anybody has it we all have it. Hey, if I caught my son with that stuff I would bag him quicker than I would anyone else. I'd bag him first. If I knew it was in my house, I wouldn't send for the city police, I'd send for the narcs, and they could have him. He'd be gone—gee oh enn ee. It's sick, disgusting, debasing, dehumanizing."

Having entered something called the Explosive Anchorage—a piece of the river where ships wait for berths at the maritime port of Guayaquil—Stella gives up her thrusting and slowly glides to a stop. Bank to bank, the width here is nearly a mile. Beside the water is little solid ground, just mangrove swamp: the *manglar*. In one place there is firmness enough to support three tin shacks on stilts.

Otherwise the river on either side is backlashed with vegetation, impenetrable—concealing in wilderness the seaport that is around two bends and less than five miles away. Now, after all the talk of world piracy from the Strait of Malacca to the Bight of Benin, after the crescendo of pirate stories aboard this ship as we have come ever farther up the Guayas River, we have again reached the war-zone front, the precincts of Guayaquil. The bosun has assembled the A.B.s and ordinaries of the idle watches. They are spread around the deck like an army. The slower the ship moves, the greater the tension grows. The anchor is about to go down. Louis Smothers, in his Queen Mary cap, says, "I ain't going to put a fire hose on nobody's child. You do that and they'll send your name up and down the coast. They'll break your legs. And when you go in the hospital this ship will sail on with its cargo. When you're lying in the hospital, the doctors and the nurses will finish you off."

Jim Gossett the electrician, tall and scant, who looks like an old ranch hand with his frayed jeans and weathered face, says, with a wild glint in his eye, "I'm a company man. I save the cargo."

Murray the ordinary says, "I'm going to the stern. If anyone comes up there, I'll point the way. I'll tell him where to go."

Pirogues have collected on the port side. Some call them beggar boats. There are four, and one is a dugout. Paddlers, facing each other, are in the bows and sterns, holding position in the current with hand-carved paddles. Other people ride in the middle, with fold-open nets to catch the bars of soap, the cans of Coca-Cola, the bags of cookies that are raining down from the ship. Calvin King buys cookies at the duty-free shops in Balboa to throw to these people in Guayaquil. Skippers warn one another that the people in these pirogues could be the accomplices of pirates, here to create a diversion. There are children, old women, middle-aged men, a dog. In the bow of one boat is a supple young woman in red—red skirt, white blouse, red jacket, bare feet. Graham Ramsay says, "I wonder if she got my allotment check."

Trevor Procter retorts, "It wouldn't be the first time that someone got an allotment check from two people."

A heaving line comes floating down the river and is picked up by the people in the dugout. Procter says, "That's our line!" On a transceiver he calls the bosun: "Hey, bose, I see your heaving line floating down the river."

The bosun tells him to notify the mate.

Pirates have boarded the ship, evidently up the anchor chain and through the hawsepipe to the fo'c'sle deck. How many of them? Where are they now? Who knows?

Understand: this ship is about the length of the Port Authority Bus Terminal, Rockefeller Center, Pennsylvania Station, Union Square. To berth her you need almost three city blocks. With her piled-high containers divided by canyons under the jumbo boom, she is, if nothing else, labyrinthine. She carries a crew of thirty-four. Thirty-four highly trained SWAT troops would have a hard time defending Rockefeller Center, so what can be expected of a militia of aging gourds? Moreover, there's so much of the ship and so few of them that the ship might as well be an open city. Action that occurs at Fifty-third Street escapes all notice at Fifty-sixth.

Confusion therefore occurs and follows. Fast-crackling rifle shots. Bullets slamming the mangroves. A pirogue full of pirates fleeing for the swamps, pursued by more bullets.

Very powerful boats appear. One of them circles the ship. Two lingering pirates cling to the bills of the anchor not in use. They stand on the flukes. They plunge into the river. Swiftly receding in the brown current, their heads bob. Their heads become dots in the water as they are swept away.

The pirates' forty-horse pirogue, with stores seized from the upper forepeak, reaches a sandspit at the edge of the *manglar*. There are six aboard. They take off, running.

An official launch from Guayaquil, making no apparent adjustment to the turn of events, comes alongside, business as usual: the port agent, the port officers, the necessary papers—the process known as clearing a ship. Short-sleeved, bureaucratic, the visitors climb the gangway from the launch. Smiles. Greetings. *Con mucho gusto. Encantado. Muy amigo mío.* Evidently, nothing that has occurred in the last fifteen minutes has surprised them, or even much interested them. They go into the thwartships passage. They follow one another up stairways to the boat deck. Captain Washburn descends from the bridge to meet them. The captain is in dress whites, white shoes. A .38 revolver is tucked in the back of his belt. The port agent hands him manifests and mail.

After a time, the powerful boat that was circling the ship pulls up at the bottom of the gangway. Sprawled on the floorboards are two wet prisoners with black bags over their heads. Their wrists are tied behind their backs. These were the swimmers who dived from the anchor flukes. The powerboat has a crew of four. Two of them carry .45s, another a shotgun. They wear sports shirts and ordinary trousers—nowhere a uniform, not a clue in the clothing to who is who or means to do what. A short, trim, serious man about thirty years of age comes up the gangway with a .45 tucked in his belt and under his unbuttoned shirt. If you are standing there beside him when he steps on the deck, you can be pardoned if you wonder who he is. Does he know those prisoners? Are the prisoners a ruse? Is he the pirate king? In the center of his finely structured and handsome face—set like a gem in one of his front teeth—is a gold star. He says that he is a naval officer. A colleague joins him. They ask to see the captain.

Captain Washburn is informed by walkie-talkie, "These two say they are active-duty Navy men, but they are wearing no uniforms and are walking around the main deck with cocked .45s."

Washburn says, "That's the best uniform I know."

Scarce has this exchange occurred when the Guayaquil port officials reappear in the thwartships passage and, with nothing more than a frank glance at the trussed and hooded pirates, file down the gangway to their launch. Each port official carries two cartons of cigarettes and a six-pack of Coca-Cola. In the slop chest of the Stella Lykes there are many cigarettes and much cola for the visits of port officials. Sometimes they hand back unfiltered cigarettes and ask for filters.

The day settles down in the Explosive Anchorage. The Navy men patrol the main deck. Captain Washburn, in his office, pauses to read his mail. I leave the group of crewmen at the head of the gangway, go through the thwartships passage, and walk the starboard side. One of the Navy men is there—the one with the star in his incisor. He is intently watching the mangrove shore. He has seen six men shuttling among the plants, making their way toward the tin shacks. Around my neck is an eight-power monocular on a nylon cord. With a sweep of the *manglar*, I see them, too. He asks if he may borrow the glass. I lift the cord and drape it around his neck, tiptoeing away from the .45. He watches the walking pirates. He asks me to report them to the captain, so the captain can, in turn, radio the port.

Washburn, at his desk in his dress whites, is smoking a cigar. "Our security forces have seen a party of pirates on the beach," he says into a transceiver, and goes back to his mail. Ordinarily, Captain Washburn is not a smoker of anything. He bites off and lights up only when the Washington Redskins have won a football game. He looks down fondly at the letter before him. It contains the name of a new human being: Zachary David Howell. Jacqueline has written to the captain, "Smoke a cigar. Your great-grandson is at least as good as the Redskins."

As evening closes in on the four-to-eight watch, cargo lights have been hung off the main deck, brightening the surrounding water. Andy is on the bridge. Mac and Calvin are deployed on deck, on patrol. At 5 P.M., Calvin calls on his transceiver to say that all is well. The anchorage is quiet. No apparent pirates. Andy calls Mac.

"Are you still alive and kickin'?"

"No. Just kickin'."

Mac has been posted to the fantail, where he sits on a chair under the American flag and sends his eyes on patrol. The sun is down and the river dark long before the end of the watch. In his lap is a flashlight.

"Who gave you the flashlight?" I ask him.

He answers, "The mate."

"What are you going to do with it?"

"Shine it in the eyes of the banditos, then drop it and run."

With his flashlight and his transceiver, he looks like a night watchman. "When you come down to this bandito country, you take your life in your hands," he says. "The people here—they treat this ship like a chicken. They pluck it whenever they wish. Why do I carry all this stuff? If the banditos attack, I am going to run anyway."

It was here on the fantail that the two sailors were tied up at knifepoint on the earlier voyage. This has made Calvin especially nervous. The crew on patrol carry no weapons. They are now supported, however, by six guards hired from shore who are armed with 16-gauge shotguns and are spread about the decks under the leadership of an Ecuadorian marine. Their headgear fails to suggest the equator. One guard is wearing a thick wool ski cap. Others wear balaclavas, with candy stripes and white tassels. Like knights' helmets, the balaclavas are drawn down to cover the lower face and the chin, leaving only slits for the guards' eyes. The air temperature is around eighty, the relative humidity sixty-two per cent. A guard in a chair politely shifts his gun so that it ceases to point at my knees. The guns are loaded not with shot but with large lead slugs. To one of the guards David Carter says, in Spanish, "If you miss the pirates, you'll sink the boat."

In being a merchant mariner, there is danger enough without pirates. A couple of days ago, Mac took hold of a ladder rail and it came off in his hand, rusted rotten. The ladder led from the fo'c'sle deck to the cabin deck, at the extreme port side. The ship was in a deep roll. Mac looked over his shoulder and straight down to the green sea. He was virtually hanging over the side. He struggled through another roll, teetered, and remained aboard. At Ascension Island some years ago, he was painting the hull of a tanker from a small boat that was lifted by a swell and driven underwater as it smashed against the ship. Just in time, he leaped free.

"I almost lost my life. There were fish of every denomination in that water."

Men fall down hatches on merchant ships: a hatch cover may be ajar; they walk over an open edge and are killed by the long fall into the hold. On diesel ships, you breathe heavy fumes. You fight diesel fires. Near diesel engines, you wear ear covers or you are stone-deaf within a year. In Stella's engine room, David Carter always has a hand on a rail. He says there's an unwritten rule: "One hand for the *load* and one hand for your*self*." David got his first job after a guy going down a ladder fell and broke his leg. "You'll *notice* a lot of guys in the engine room have *burns* all over them. It doesn't take much—just a little *jolt*. You hit a *steam* line and you got a nasty *scar*." Bill Boone, a utility man in the galley, says that he was on a Victory ship some years ago when he saw a mooring line snap and do so much damage that four amputations were required. And a funeral. The line, contracting, drew an ordinary seaman into a Panama chock and killed him. A Panama chock is a large square eye that mooring lines pass through. During a voyage to North Europe while Andy was on the tanker Potomac, the bosun tore up his knee in a fall, a line snapped and broke another man's arm, a winch tore open a pumpman's arm and crushed it from shoulder to wrist, an ordinary seaman fractured his skull walking through a watertight door, and the cook fell to the deck hallucinating, writhing, and babbling incoherently after rupturing his spleen. On the Prudential Lines' LASH Pacifico, the chief mate once performed an appendectomy in the middle of the North Atlantic while a doctor spoke to him by radio, telling him what to do. There is a service called Amver provided by the Coast Guard—Automated Mutual-Assistance Vessel Rescue System. Before your ship sails, you file a voyage plan, and it is updated in a central computer while the voyage proceeds. When a spleen ruptures, the computer locates every ship within two hundred miles of you, displays on your screen a list of the paramedics aboard them, and says what ships (if any) are carrying doctors.

On through the night we lie at anchor in a pool of festooned light, abristle with shotguns, braced for attack, and awaiting the call to a berth. It comes on the four-to-eight, in the predawn. We have little to leave in Guayaquil. The last time we ran the gantlet here, a fortnight ago, the pirates missed, among other things, five hundred VCRs. They missed half a ton of photographic supplies, three tons of plastic tape, five tons of synthetic rubber, twenty tons of crude talc, forty tons of tinplate, and three hundred tons of drilling mud. They missed five thousand six hundred barrels of resin. They missed a container said to contain seven tons of mixed windshield wipers, hubcaps, and musical jewel boxes. They missed the container said to contain sixteen thousand six hundred and thirty-six pounds of shower curtains, telephones, and wall clocks. They missed a container said to contain seventy-seven cases of bathroom locks, and four containers said to contain twenty-four thoroughbreds.

We laid all that on the dock and went to Valparaiso. From Valparaiso to Guayaquil we have brought phosphates, automobile tires, and veterinary medicine. There is a full day's work for the longshoremen, though, as we pick up seven hundred sacks of goosefoot, ninety drums of passion-fruit juice, a hundred and eighty-two thousand board feet of balsa wood, and one million four hundred thousand pounds of coffee. We pick up thirty-two empty containers. That is one of the differences between container and break-bulk freight: you have to move the empties. For transporting what may amount to about a hundred million cups of coffee from Ecuador to the United States the steamship company is charging the coffee people $69,486.78. This is Lykes Brothers' sip.

The waving shotguns and the tasselled balaclavas protect us through another night. We cast off at dawn. A Norwegian pineapple ship will take our berth. Mac, at the wheel, hand steering, says, "That ship is so sparkling clean you could eat off her deck."

Just the thought of a shipful of pineapples makes me very hungry. Happily would I get down on my knees and eat a chunk from a deck. A Norwegian deck. I say to Mac, "I wonder what the cook will be cooking today."

"Port ten," the pilot says.

Mac swings the wheel at a bend in the river. "Left ten," he responds. Then he says, "If he's a cook, I'm a surgeon."

We retrace our way through the Explosive Anchorage and pick up speed in the current. At five-fifty-one, Calvin arrives, takes over the wheel. He does not so much stand as droop.

Mac is a youth of fifty-eight. Calvin is sixty-one. Yesterday, Calvin's day began when he was called at three in the morning to prepare to stand what he describes as "my security watch with armed guards." For four hours, he walked the deck with his transceiver, reporting to the bridge every twenty minutes, and expecting at any moment to be attacked by pirates and lashed to a turnbuckle, as his watch partner had been a few months before. At eight, he had breakfast. At nine, he turned to for deck maintenance, chipping and painting forward of the house. He greased the topping lifts on the No. 2 and No. 3 cranes. He tidied up the shelter deck. He painted the main deck around the jumbo crane. He second-coated the davits for the gangway port and starboard. This may not have been New York, but the Ecuadorian sun was hot. After lunch, he chipped and painted from one until four, when he resumed walking the foredeck, on patrol. As evening approached, he spent more than an hour crawling under catwalks between hatches to find electrical outlets in which to plug the cargo lights meant to keep pirates away. At 8 P.M., when the watch ended, he went into Guayaquil with the port agent and called North Carolina, in his concern over the health of his father-in-law—"my wife's daddy"—who is ninety-two years old and is in the hospital. He returned to the ship and fell into bed at midnight. At three, he was awakened for the four-to-eight watch. Now he stands at the wheel, worried more than ever about his wife's daddy, looking for the moment almost ninety-two himself, paint-spattered from shirt to shoes, posture caving toward the letter S, a wire loose behind his hearing aid, his white cap no longer clean, his outsized bluejeans scuffing the deck. He admits defeat. He says, "I'm pretty well rest-broken now."

Calvin and Mac would be paid their usual $135.68 apiece for that exacting day painting and patrolling in Guayaquil. McLaughlin remarks as he prepares to go below, "Eighteen hours a day for decent take-home pay."

The ship carries considerable cash, so that the crew, en route, can draw what they need. In a small office on the cabin deck, Mac came upon fifteen hundred dollars one day, left there by mistake after a draw. He carried it upstairs and gave it to the captain.

It is 6 A.M. in the Republic of the Equator. The twentieth of August. Sixty-eight degrees. The Woermann Wakamba is coming up the river. We will pass her port to port. She flies the flag of Panama and has a big white bone in her teeth. This large bow wave, spreading to the sides, is followed by another wave, some distance back. If you measure the length of the bow wave—the distance from the first wave to the second—you can tell how fast a ship is going. The distance in this case is two hundred and twenty-five feet. How do I know? I'm guessing. It's a convenient guess, because 1.1 times the square root of the length of the wave equals the speed of the ship in knots. The Woermann Wakamba is doing better than sixteen knots. She draws a big sea. Ships can make surf even at sixteen knots.

We are disturbing someone's breakfast. As the Stella Lykes and the Woermann Wakamba pass each other port to port, each is passing a third vessel, inconsiderable in the river: a needle boat, a pirogue, under a homemade sail. There are three men in it. One is wearing a jacket and tie. There is a campfire in the boat, with food cooking on it, sending up flavored smoke.

A few good campfires might loosen up the mealtimes on the Stella. I remember the first time I appeared in the officers' dining room for dinner. The captain was there, and Andy Chase, and Bernie Tibbotts. All three had been served and were eating. No one else was present. Tibbotts sat alone at a table, facing a wall. Chase sat alone at a table, facing the opposite wall. The captain, at his table, sat with his back to a third wall, looking into the room, and into the space between the turned backs of Chase and Tibbotts. Franz Kafka was up in the ceiling, crawling on a fluorescent tube. No one spoke. No one so much as nodded when I came in. I sat down where I was supposed to: at a fourth table, across the room from the captain. I looked at him through the slot between the other men's backs. I did not have—I'm here to tell you—the temerity to speak.

Each of these tables, mind, is large enough to accommodate four or more people, but you know your place and you eat in it. When food is set before you, you gulp it and go. "The invariable maxim is to throw away all politeness —that is, never to wait for each other, and bolt off the minute one has done eating," says Darwin. He is describing the crew of the Stella Lykes. They eat like sled dogs. They do speak, occasionally. There is no hostility. They mean it when they say that to sail with this captain is to sail on a happy ship. I have walked into the dining room when only two people were there, each facing a different wall. Without looking around, they were conversing. But primarily they are in the dining room to eat, not talk, in the finest restaurant in downtown Catatonia.

The unlicensed crewmen waste no time eating, either. Their dining room is on the other side of the galley. Like the officers, the unlicensed are waited on. Like the officers, they have tablecloths. The menu is the same. The one difference is that if you're an officer you wipe your lips with a cloth napkin; if you're unlicensed, you use paper.

About the food—it can be confirmed that Mac is not a surgeon. At lunch, there are three entrées, at dinner four, revolving through time in fixed cycles, like the navigational stars. When flounder fillets compete with pork hocks, short ribs, and Texas-style tamales, the choice is neither simple nor obvious. The grilled strip-loin steaks cannot be said to have an advantage over their traditional rivals—broiled franks, American chop suey, and fried mah-chena egg rolls. Prime ribs compete uncertainly with smoked sausage, Cantonese-style fried rice, and East Indian lamb curry. Each day's menu includes seventy items, none fresh (in the sense that everything is bought in the United States and stored for the voyage). The pork chops may be cobblestones, the salmon steak taxidermy. The honeycomb tripe may be used to stop a hole in the hull. Virtually written into the scrambled eggs with brains is the question: Which are the brains? But the turnips, the turnip greens, the black-eyed peas, the pinto beans, the roast lamb, roast pork, roast veal, roast turkey, the kippers, the catfish, the ham and grits, the eggplant, the hush puppies, the brisket, the ice creams, the boiled smoked ox tongue with mustard sauce do not deserve to be called inedible. They tend to explain why so many in the crew have the silhouettes of shucked clams.

At breakfast one Saturday (day of the green-onion omelette), Captain Washburn slowed the pace of eating with a disquisition to his tablemates on the batting techniques of Rogers Hornsby. The captain, who seems to remember everything he has ever read, heard, or seen, may know only a little less about Rogers Hornsby than he does about Sammy Baugh. He knows that Hornsby hit .397 in 1921, the highest batting average in the National League since 1899. He knows that Hornsby hit .424 in 1924 and that his fielding percentage in the same year was .965. He laid all this out, or something like it, for the chief mate, the chief engineer, and the radio operator, who sit at table with him. Bill Beach, the radio operator, listened with apparent interest, and after Hornsby's far-from-the-plate, choke-and-crouch batting stance had been anatomized all the way out through the metacarpals and into the phalanges Beach asked if a baseball glove is made of leather or rubber. He also asked—out of the blue—what team Joe DiMaggio played for. In the Merchant Marine generally, the person they call Sparks is regarded as the occupant of a numbered cloud, a distinct, if not strange, well-paid weirdo. Vernon McLaughlin tells of a radio operator who would not smoke a cigarette unless someone else had smoked it first, a radio operator who burst into tears every morning on the bridge, and a radio operator who ate raw garlic cloves as if they were salted peanuts. William Raymond Charteris Beach, radio operator of the Stella Lykes, is not on any kind of cloud; he is merely Scottish. He grew up in Edinburgh, and he doesn't know Rogers Hornsby from Donald Ban MacCrimmon. Beach used to work for the daily *Scotsman*, transmitting and receiving radio pictures. As a former journalist, he is not comfortable with the fact that the crews of American merchant ships crisscross the oceans with little or no idea of what is happening ashore. Voluntarily, in his spare time, he writes and publishes a one-page all-caps daily newspaper, which he circulates through the house. The name of the paper has changed three times on this voyage. It has been the *Sun Sentinel*, the *Sun Reporter*, the *World News*, and the *Knowledge Nugget*. His wire service is wireless. Among other things, this is what has been happening ashore:

CHILD KILLER SET TO GO TO THE CHAIR FOR KILLING HIS 8 YEAR OLD NIECE.

DOW JONES 2131.

HARVARD CLOSED DUE TO HEAT WAVE.

YEN 133 = $1.

L.A.—GANG WARS—3 KILLED AND 4 WOUNDED.

DETROIT—ON A CAR BUMPER STICKER:—"ON A QUIET NIGHT YOU CAN HEAR A FORD RUST."

NIXON SAYS—IT WAS OK FOR QUAILS RELATIVES TO PULL STRINGS.

TEL A VIV—HOUSE WIFE KILLED A ROACH AND THREW IT INTO A TOILET. BUG STILL ALIVE, SO SHE SPRAYED A FULL CAN OF BUG SPRAY INTO THE BOWL. HUSBAND CAME HOME, USED TOILET, LIT A CIGARETTE, FUMES CAUGHT FIRE, BURNED HIS SENSITIVE PARTS, MEDICS CAME, PUT HIM ON A STRETCHER, ASKED WHAT HAPPENED, STARTED LAUGHING, DROPPED HIM, BROKE HIS PELVIS & 2 WRISTS.

1100 POUNDS OF COKE FROM A HAITIAN FREIGHTER, 7 PEOPLE ARRESTED.

100 YEARS AGO TODAY—WILD BILL HICKOK WAS SHOT TO DEATH AFTER GETTING THE DEAD MAN'S HAND OF ACES AND 8'S.

"In Deadwood, South Dakota," Captain Washburn was heard to mutter. "Shot in Deadwood, South Dakota, by Black Jack McCall. Not in a man-to-man. They went up behind him."

To combat boredom, Andy takes his guitar with him

on most voyages. He goes up on the bow or out on the fantail to be off by himself and sing. Or he goes to his cabin. He says, "I close my door and sing my heart out."

To defeat boredom—or something—a third engineer on the previous voyage brought pornographic videos with him. Almost every night, he took a pillow and a blanket to the officers' lounge and spent eight hours watching the movies. Lykes Brothers supplies videocassettes with less vivid ratings. There are twelve movies in a steel drawer in the so-called IBM Room, on the cabin deck, where the ship's computer is. (A Navy ship half the size of ours will typically carry three hundred movies.) On the drawer is a sign that reads "Proclamation—Within Find Movies and Condoms for Your Pleasure." The sign includes a drawing of a mortar and pestle decorated with the letters Rx. At the beginning of the voyage, Captain Washburn wrote a note to crew members which said, in part, "Prostitutes, even those professionals who carry health cards, are not routinely checked for AIDS virus in South America. AIDS is not curable at this time! AIDS will kill you!! At this time the safest known way to avoid contacting AIDS, when engaging in sex, is to use a condom (rubber). To that end a supply of condoms (rubbers) is available on a 24 hours basis in the IBM Room in the draw with the movies. You are not limited to a specific number nor do you need anyone's permission to help yourself to the supply. Simply take what you need."

The crew, by and large, are not self-conscious about the sex they have ashore. You could not even call them candid, unless it is also candid to mention, say, that you took your car in for a job at Midas Muffler. In Lima, one crewman visits a prostitute who is also a certified public accountant but can't make ends meet as a C.P.A. In Buenaventura, he needs a new cliental arrangement, because his friend of two years is pregnant.

In the era of the Vietnam Sealift, the Merchant Marine had a much higher percentage of boozers and junkies than are now on the oceans under the American flag. Crews are reduced. There are few ships. The jobs that are now so hard to come by can be permanently lost: seamen can get on the "Do Not Reemploy" list. "After Lykes, there aren't too many places to go anymore," Washburn remarked one day. "And if the company is tolerant of a drug-related incident the Coast Guard may not be."

When I said that I was not able to sense drug use in the house, the captain looked at the ceiling and threw lariats with his eyes. He said, "No doubt we have users around here. People who smoke a few things. I don't think we have any mainliners or anybody really strung out. You can't put this many people together and not have somebody using something."

The late Moore-McCormack Lines used to permit officers' wives to accompany their husbands on voyages. Generally speaking, that is not done in the United States Merchant Marine but is customary on European ships. The Lykes Brothers' Cygnus, which was built by Germans for their own merchant fleet, has a swimming pool, an exercise room, and related spaces that do not exist on American freighters and tankers. There are a few exceptions, but, as

Bill Beach has said, "American ships compared to European ships are a disgrace. The design is better in European ships. They're like homes. There are bigger rooms. There are drapes and French doors in the lounge. This ship's equipment is antique compared with Japanese or German ships. Norwegian ships are immaculate. They have wine at dinner."

Andy's cabin, on the cabin deck, is nine and a half by fifteen feet, bathroom and shower included. Usually, second mates live in that space eighty-four days. If their wives were aboard, they would do well to bring their lawyers. On the other hand, the age of the seabag is long over. A mariner can get on the ship with five suitcases if he wants to. Some people bring their computers. One flight down from the cabin deck is the upper deck, home of the unlicensed. The word "fo'c'sle" has gravitated to this part of the house. Mac and Calvin are in cabins side by side, each door marked "4-8 A.B." Each man's cabin is five feet six inches wide and fourteen feet deep, and has a desk with three drawers, a sink, and two more drawers under the bunk. The two cabins have a common bathroom, or, in Calvin's words, "shower and commode with watch partner." Around a corner of the narrow corridor is David Carter the demac. His cabin is seven by eleven, with a sink alcove. Above the pictures of his kids is a poster of a seminude woman who could be made of titanium. Every sailor has at least one porthole. David's looks out at containers.

Some ships supply individual refrigerators in people's rooms. On this ship, only the chiefs have them. Air-conditioning became standard on American merchant ships in the nineteen-seventies. There is a union rule that linen must be changed every day if the air-conditioning breaks down. "When you see Third World junkers," Andy says, "all the portholes are open." The quarters of the bosun are in the rear center of the house, the chief engineer in the left front corner, the chief mate in the right front corner, the captain above the chief mate, and Sparks highest of all—on the bridge deck, in crescent-shaped quarters within the false stack. There are four rooms for passengers, not all occupied. On many voyages they run empty. Carlos, the trainer of Dr. Sab, was in one. The author Alex Haley is noted for riding on merchant ships as a way of isolating himself from distractions and forcing himself to write. He could write a book called "Routes." Our most durable passenger is Milian Engh, of Edinboro, Pennsylvania, who, with his wife, Gretchen, has travelled on merchant ships many times and has come now despite the inconveniences of an all-out battle with cancer. He has lost the roof of his mouth, and sometimes has to pinch his nostrils in order to achieve speech, but he achieves it, and then some, darting out in response to anything he looks upon as frivolous, inaccurate, or foolish. He weighs a hundred and five pounds. His all but fleshless arms are dark blue. Yet he has brought his canvases, his easel, his small wooden case of acrylic paints. His subject is the ship itself. He is painting her against a brooding jungle of his own invention.

A day or so ago, I heard John Shephard, the sailor who makes the officers' and passengers' beds, chatting up the

Enghs about death aboard ship. Gretchen cheerfully recalled a thirty-year-old woman who had a cerebral hemorrhage during a trip they made to the east coast of Africa ("They said she was all right, but they carried her off dead"), and John enumerated many fatalities, including a four-hundred-pound seaman who proved to be a difficult fit in the ship's freezer. Shephard, who is half belly and all tact, would weigh four hundred pounds himself if he were much more than five feet tall. Even his belly has a chip on it, but who could blame him? His listed next of kin is Billy Sweat, "a friend." Shephard's home is wherever Shephard happens to be. ("Georgia, Louisiana—wherever I'm at—I use a post-office box. I don't have no address.") He says he has slept on the streets and eaten out of garbage cans and dumpsters. He says, "It's a rough life. Rough life. Go ashore, you spend your money, get kicked in the tail. Plenty of friends till the money runs out. A seaman smells like a rose when he's got money, but when he has no money they say, 'Motherfucker, get another ship.' Friends gone—George Washington, Lincoln, all them other good buddies—you go to the union hall and sit and sit and sit. Might take a year. Five more years, there won't be no more Merchant Marine. It's going down the guts. You find yourself something else to do. I'm a mortician, I'm an embalmer. I don't have a license, but I do the job. And I drive am-bew-lance. And I go second engineer on a porgy boat. Snapper boats. Out of work. No ship." More than once, he has remarked that he finds things even less pleasant on shipboard. "Out chea, it's a rough life." He told me with irritation that on three separate occasions he had saved someone's life at sea but since he did not get his name in the union paper he doubted if he would ever save anybody else. He looked over my shoulder at maps I have of the ocean floor. He said, "I didn't know that was all that feet deep." He asked if I had taken the pictures from an airplane.

The remarks about shipboard deaths gave me a little shiver in the bones. When I worked for W. R. Grace & Company, in the nineteen-fifties, I was sent off on a Grace ship with a party of stockholders, one of whom was destined for the freezer. I was one of several precursive yuppies who, obeying orders, made an appearance as red Indians on the rolling deck of the Santa Rosa. With our skins painted bronze, with tomahawks in our hands, and dressed only in loincloths, we hopped in a circle, chanting, "Grow with Grace. Grow with Grace." The stockholder who died had had a choice location—a sort of crossroads cabin, close to the purser and much in the center of the fun. After her sudden death, it was thought that her cabin should be reoccupied at once, in order to dispel the pall it was casting. Two of us flipped a coin to see who would sleep in her bed.

Four P.M., August 20th, sixty miles south of the equator, this is one lovely day: air temperature seventy-four, relative humidity sixty-nine per cent, sea temperature seventy-seven. The air is so brilliant that only Vernon McLaughlin and the radar see the dense piece of apparent sky that solidifies as we pass near it—a dry and silvery pastel island. Across the wheelhouse, the captain paces and frets—head down, eyes on the deck, his thoughts so concentrated on the next hazard of the voyage that his mood is unrelieved by the present weather. In part to Andy, in part to the ship, he addresses remarks about the low-draft channel into Buenaventura, where the ship has to maneuver as if it were skywriting and the word it spells is "lawsuit."

It is no place for the inexperienced, he is saying. It is no place for unskilled labor. You wouldn't want to be going in there under a flag of convenience with a novice crew.

You simply could not get in there with novices in the engine room:

"You can't get a demac down there that's cutting these fires in and out and changing tips, and watching the water in the boilers, and watching the air regulator on these high-pressure things—that only comes with time. When something goes wrong, all of a sudden you've lost the water and you have too much air or no air, you've got too much heat here, and that fire's gone out, and you're maneuvering. All of a sudden you're dead in the water. You can run away from more trouble than you can drift away from, you know. You can't drift away from trouble; you drift into trouble. Once you've lost the plant, your maneuverability—your ability to do anything to control the situation—is gone."

Nor could you get into Buenaventura with novices on the bridge:

"You've got to have somebody up here who can steer or, hey, you're accident-prone. If there's other traffic around, it's usually a good accident. You have plowed into another ship, or another ship has plowed into you. Or if you haven't put her up in the sand you've put her up on a rock. You can pull her off the sand, but if that rock has penetrated your hull you can pull all you want. That one little rock is just like a huge spike that's just got you nailed down there, and you can have *ten* tugboats out there pulling, and you can have your engines go full astern, and you just stay there."

Once, on the way in to Buenaventura, Stella shuddered

and abruptly stopped. Captain Washburn remembers that he said at that moment, "Heavens to Murgatroyd, we're aground!" Whereupon the mate at his side went to the logbook, recorded the exact time, and wrote "Aground." The weight of this memory causes the captain to slap his forehead. He explains, "In this business, you don't write 'Aground.' You never write 'Aground'. You say, 'We have touched bottom.' If you hit a dock, you say, 'We touched the dock.' If the side is stove in and the hatches are buckling, you say, 'We touched the dock—I think.' "

In sequential turns, the mates write the logbook like monastic scribes, filling long columns with precise minutiae. A part of their job is to account for every mile steamed, every minute of the voyage. There are economic reasons for amassing data, such as computerized fuel efficiency. But the principal purpose of the endless ledger seems to be legal. The mates are floating law clerks. Voyage in, voyage out, a great deal of what they do serves no purpose beyond a thorough preparation for an appearance in admiralty court. Nowhere does the ship sail free of chimeric litigation. When we were inching at ten knots over the bar at the mouth of the Guayas, Andy recorded the exact hour, minute, and second that we passed each of many buoys there—half a mile of buoys—in case we ran agr . . . in case we touched bottom. As the ship maneuvers in every port, he or another mate records many dozens of commands and the exact moment at which each is issued, thus extending the magnitude of the brief. Andy is respectful of these requirements. He has been teaching of late at Maine Maritime Academy;

his course in seamanship and rules of the road deals with this subject. Captain Washburn remembers a second mate who was contemptuous of details. He confided to Washburn that, in effect, logbooks are playthings for Sea Scouts and maritime cadets. He said his last ship had had no logbook. Washburn said to him, "Just because they did it on the S.S. Neversink with the Whodunit Steamship Line, they're not going to do it here. Take your careless laid-back attitude and go wreck someone else."

In the chief mate's cabin is a gallery of photographs showing the present cargo—how and where it is secured and stowed. They are like photographs of residential interiors made to show the insurance company in the event of a fire. The chief mate's pictures—evolving and archival—are intended for a courtroom. The odds that they will be needed are shorter than one might think. They are less than thirty to one. The chief mate is in charge of the cargo, and that is why he so often works a twenty-hour day. If anything tumbles or spills, the Coast Guard will be looking for him.

There are strange, amphibious cases in the annals of admiralty law: the ship that hit the train, the ship that hit the Rolls-Royce. On December 25, 1984, Christmas took a place between Charybdis and Corryvreckan on the list of nautical hazards. In opposite directions, two Very Large Crude Carriers were rounding the Cape of Good Hope. Each captain altered course so the ships could draw close and the crews could exchange Christmas greetings. The ships collided.

Captain Washburn, who calls depositions "séances,"

has had legal functions to perform that cannot be called unpleasant. On the Cygnus, for example, he was once heading south toward the Florida Straits when a third assistant engineer requested permission to get married. His name was Alan Kane, and he wanted to be married aboard ship, with the captain officiating. The bride was in Maine. By radio, Captain Washburn and the town clerk of Tremont, Maine, united the couple even as the ship increased their separation. The steward of the Cygnus prepared a wedding supper. He baked a wedding cake. The ship was on its way to the Far East. The Kanes now have a daughter whose name is Shannon Cygnus.

The four-to-eight ends. The four-to-eight begins. Four A.M. in the cashmere blackness. We have entered Colombian water. Intently, Andy leans over the radar plotter, a disk of suffused illumination on the otherwise dark bridge, working with his wax pencil. Calvin, the helmsman, is leaning over the plotter, too. Andy is designing an oak table. He is designing it for Calvin. At home in North Carolina, Calvin has four oak four-by-fours that he will turn into legs, and he says he wants a two-inch top. Andy recommends a one-inch top.

We have entered, also, the doldrums. The lovely atmosphere has slipped behind us. Now even the night air is sticky. It is windless, and is moved only by the ship. Andy remarks that the skipper of a tall ship once told him that everyone should spend at least twenty-four hours becalmed, just to see what it is like. "You can sustain more damage in calms than in gales," Andy says. "A boat rocks endlessly back and forth with no wind to steady her. A ship flips back and forth, snapping things. The heavy air doesn't move. Everything is stuffy, muggy, and totally sticky below."

"That sounds like my house in New Jersey."

"Your house doesn't rock back and forth."

"Not anymore."

The horse latitudes, which shift seasonally and lie between prevailing winds, are also calm. Becalmed ships—completely out of corn, cereal, bread, hay, barley, oats, apples, and anything else a horse might eat—sometimes had to throw livestock overboard in the horse latitudes.

With daylight, the captain is in the wheelhouse, muttering, "One of these days, something amiss is going to happen in Buenaventura. A combination of current, bad pilots, little dock space, and so forth is going to ding a ship." At eighteen knots, we bring Buenaventura into view—a few mid-rise buildings among thousands of shanties compressed on a small peninsula in jumbled profusion, like laundry spread over rocks at the side of a stream. Bill Beach has described Buenaventura as "a cesspool of whorehouses and bars." Vernon McLaughlin has called it "*the* romance port." The River Anchicayá emerges from the jungle here. To get to our berth we must cross its bar and follow its sinuous channel. We are drawing twenty-four feet ten inches with our present cargo. The Fathometer shows no measurable gap between the hull and the bottom as we cross the bar. In front of the town, the ship describes an S in the channel. "We turn tighter to port because we have a right-hand screw," Washburn says. "From one ship to the next, you never know. I guess that's why they call them her and she, because they go any which way."

The berth we are headed for comes into view. It is the middle one of three beside a long wharf, and in the two other berths ships are tied up. The bow of the one and the stern of the other are separated by seven hundred feet. Stella will need ninety-five per cent of that space. A thirty-five-foot margin divides Washburn from a ding. The pilot's nonchalance is in inverse proportion to his experience. Reflected in the pilot's eyes Washburn can see a courtroom full of lawyers. Tugboats churn around the ship. They lack experience, too. Until recently, tugs were not included in the services of this port.

As Stella inches forward, the captain watches over the pilot as he might over one of his great-grandchildren attempting to ride a bicycle for the first time. And he says to the rest of us, "This ship probably handled better before it was stretched than it does now. They made it a hundred and fifteen feet longer, and they added greatly to the gross tonnage. So you're pushing a lot more ship and a lot more weight through the water. On top of that, you have the same propeller, engine, and rudder characteristics that she had when she was a smaller ship—not only smaller but with a different hull configuration, which means different power curves. With more ship and the same rudder, she probably does not answer the helm as quickly as she did when she was smaller. She still answers the helm well at high rates of speed. At low rates of speed—when you're maneuvering, dead slow, and slow, and when the ship is dead in the water, to pick it up—that's where she is sluggish, and that's where you'd like a higher degree of maneuverability. But you don't have it, so that is something that you take in mind when you are handling this particular ship. Also, she does not back down strong immediately. If you're approaching a situation and you're coming in too fast, you cannot count on your engines going astern to pull you out of it. You have to allow a little extra time. She backs down strong once she grabs, once she gets ahold of it. You have to take that into consideration when you're maneuvering or coming up to a dock. You cannot count on the engines to pull you out of it if you're coming in at too high a rate of speed."

"How long does it take her to grab?" I ask him.

"A minute or two. But a minute or two is a lifetime in this business. You're down to seconds sometimes. A minute can be an eternity. But when she does grab she will back down strong, and she will pull the ship astern. The thing to do is not to be going too fast in the first place, yet you have to keep a certain amount of way on her to have rudder control and maneuverability, because if you go too slow she doesn't answer the helm. There isn't a bow thruster on her, as there is on most modern ships. They didn't put one on when they stretched her."

When Washburn was skipper of the Sue Lykes, he found an overturned ship in Indonesian waters with her captain and four remaining crewmen standing on the hull, where they had been for eighty-four hours. Numerous ships had reached the scene, but the weather was so wild that no one could achieve a rescue. Washburn maneuvered for an hour, and docked his ship beside the upturned hull. For this feat he was later summoned by the United Seamen's Service to the Grand Ballroom of the Waldorf-Astoria, where he was elevated to the honorary rank of Admiral of the Ocean Seas. Now, in Buenaventura, the admiral decides to dock the ship himself, to ignore the hurt feelings of the pilot, to keep at a safe distance the incompetent tugs and reduce their crews to spectators, to rely on his own eye and his commands through the engine-order telegraph to solve this problem in very tight large-scale parallel parking. As an automobile driver, he may not know where he is. To watch him as a golfer, though, is to notice that the closer he gets to the pin the abler and more precise he becomes. Which of these characteristics will predominate here remains to be seen. His commands fall like rain, and in the same steady rhythm, with no revisions. With a few adjusting motions fore and aft, he goes into his berth as if he were closing a drawer. Leaning over the bridge wing, he looks down at the dockside and sees fifteen inches of water. He straightens up. "Nice job," he says. "I couldn't have done it better myself."

We brought very little cargo to Buenaventura, but we did bring the crew. We had eighteen thousand pounds of powdered graphite, twenty tons of used auto parts, ninety-one tons of polypropylene for making plastic furniture, ten tons of tiremaking-machinery parts, and two Ford trucks, but scarcely was the first of it in the air and dangling from cables over the dock when the gangway rattled with springy feet and the streets were full of sailors and mates. Everyone was looking his best—clean clothes, scrubbed bodies, hair in place for the school prom. Buenaventura calls itself the Pearl of the Pacific. The crew were in a nacreous mood. An A.B. waved a happy hand. In it was a fistful of condoms.

Through the narrow streets, past tables of fruit, they homed in quickly on the Bamboo Bar, where the drinks were on them, the noise hung heavy, and attractive strangers took them away. Some came back to the ship with names and addresses. From North America they would send presents. Some came back with a passionate desire to learn Spanish. In New York they would buy Berlitz cassettes.

While the ship was berthed in Buenaventura, a woman appeared in the thwartships passage with glancing dark eyes that would melt wax. She was a slender mestiza in a green jumpsuit. She was so disconcerting that Andy later described her as tall, and the captain called her "petite." The captain also remarked in praise of her, "Her jumpsuit wasn't sprayed on." Aided by the cargo boss, a port official, she had walked up the gangway past the deck watch and past Colombian guards. The smile she threw at Andy left his shadow on the deck. She had on her mind something like Eurodollars. She spoke through an interpreter (the cargo boss), and the cargo boss said to the captain, "I am here to service your every need."

The captain said, "I guess you've never seen it all."

The cargo boss said, "I am offering my services for the duration of your stay."

The captain threw her off the ship.

The log shows that one of the sailors returned to the ship in Buenaventura "in a state of utter intoxication, unable to walk or stand." The captain threw him off the ship, too. Second offense. Sent him home by air. "Give anyone a break once," said the chief mate. "After that, he's going to get what he's got coming to him."

When the sailor had returned to the ship, he sat on a chair near the top of the gangway and would not budge. Covered, as he was, with tattoos, he looked like a melting stained-glass window. The mate asked him what his trouble was, and he said, "My toe."

The mate said, "Let's go below and have a look at it."

The sailor refused, and kept on refusing until the mate gave him the choice of seeing a doctor or going to his cabin. The sailor chose the doctor but refused to move. He was carried down the gangway in a Stokes litter. An ambulance took him to a hospital, where he tried unsuccessfully to bribe a doctor to say that he wasn't drunk and to recommend that he not work for two days. Discharging himself from the hospital, the sailor walked the streets barefoot and shirtless, and eventually found the ship. He was "repatriated medically" by the captain, who thereby gave him a second break. People ashore seem to fall into two principal categories with respect to their awareness of the United States Merchant Marine: those who have no idea what it is, and those who look upon it as the main chapter of alcoholics anadromous. On the Stella Lykes, in the many weeks of the voyage, the story of the sailor in the Stokes litter was the only story of its kind. By Coast Guard rules, alcoholic drinks are "strictly forbidden on any ship of the United States Merchant Marine." It is probable that beer and booze are on every ship of the U.S. Merchant Marine, as the world would infer in months to follow after the ship of a drinking skipper was wrecked in Alaska. Who is drinking and when are separate and significant questions. On the bridge of the Stella Lykes nothing ever suggested that anyone there had been drinking, with a single exception: after a night's sleep after Lima, one of the eight-to-twelve helmsmen remarked that he had "the big head." Captain Washburn drinks fruit juice. He swills black coffee and is totally abstinent, afloat and ashore. When he loses his sense of direction in his own driveway, he is, among other things, sober.

David Carter and I hailed a taxi in downtown Buenaventura and took a four-hour ride into the mountains, where we were stopped at gunpoint, told to lean—palms flat—against the taxi, and frisked from ankles to armpits with no politesse at the crotch. Between Buenaventura and the high country, there are two roads, and one is an unpaved single track. We wanted to see the jungle rising to the Cordillera Occidental, and we chose the single track. It went up the Valley of the Anchicayá, crossing and recrossing the stream until the gorge walls became so high that we followed an edge of the canyon rim. We passed isolated houses surrounded with bananas. We passed a half-built dugout canoe. We did not see another car for an hour at a time. David said that we were riding in a Japanese vehicle made in Colombia and called a Chevrolet. Whatever it was, it did not have a lot of clearance. It kept pounding on rock in the middle of the road. David might have preferred his bicycle, which accompanies him on ships wherever he goes. He keeps it in the shelter deck and carries it down the gangway into seaports, where it masks his identity and creates a protective effect: "Any person on a bicycle is automatically a native." In Guayaquil, he bought brake pads and a Chinese bell.

With altitude, the country opened out into long Andean vistas, across the deeply dissected vegetal terrain. We went around promontories and into reentrants, around more promontories, more reentrants, and suddenly came to three soldiers—or men who were dressed as soldiers—waving us to a stop with Israeli-made automatic weapons. David recognized the guns as Galils. He recognized them from an eight-hundred-page catalogue he had picked up at Uncle Sal's gun shop in Miami and carries with him on the ship. When David was a student at Tulane University, in New Orleans, he drove to Auburn, Alabama, to see his girlfriend Betty There. (In New Orleans he had a girlfriend, of the same name, whom he called Betty Here.) On the way to Auburn, he experienced trouble with his car and stopped to correct it. A car drew up. Four men got out. David thought, This is nice of them to stop to help me. They were carrying tire irons, however, and they demanded his money. Obligingly, he pulled out from under his shirt a Colt .41 revolver, which his father—an electrical contractor with fifteen trucks—had given him with just such an emergency in mind. He pointed the Colt between the eyes of the man closest to him and said, "I'll give you ten seconds to get out of here before I start shooting. One . . . two . . . three . . ." As he counted, the robbers got into their car. When he reached ten, however, the car had not moved. As a way of starting it up, he shot out the rear window. The wheels screeched, leaving rubber on the road. David emptied the revolver.

"By now they were all on the floor," he said, telling the story. "I think they got the message."

Fortunately, the soldiers in the mountains were real. They were guarding a hydroelectric station that was out of sight below us. The mountains were full of guerrillas, attacking somewhere every day. Just as the guerrillas (or, for that matter, common bandits) could dress as soldiers, they could also travel as tourists in a Japanese Chevrolet.

After the incident, when I expressed annoyance at having been frisked by armed soldiers, David said quickly, "It's no different in Florida. If the police see a Mercedes or BMW moving under the speed limit with a black or Hispanic face in it, they call that a 'profile' and they pull it over."

The young Buenaventuran who was driving us was unfamiliar with the mountain valleys, and as more dirt roads began to converge in tracts of chocolate and coffee he became essentially lost. At that moment, the top of the gangway on the Stella Lykes—where the sailing board gave notice of an evening departure—seemed a thousand miles away, while in fact it was less than a hundred. We drove almost aimlessly for thirty minutes more and finally came to a sign:

AFRODISIACOS 50 M

We had found civilization.

At a newsstand in Buenaventura, on our way back to the ship, we bought a copy of the Cali *El País*. The headline of the lead story said: "GUERRILLA ASALTÓ 89 VEHÍCULOS." Guerrillas dressed as soldiers had attacked and robbed eighty-nine cars and buses in the mountains. But that was the day before.

In Buenaventura, we picked up one million one hundred thousand pounds of coffee, fifteen hundred cartons of lollipops, twenty tons of edible gelatin, and Andy's father, Epes (Dick) Chase, who had never gone through the Panama Canal and joined the ship to do so. We picked up four thousand cartons of Quaker Oats, four hundred and thirty-six cartons of glass Nativity scenes, eleven hundred and ninety-six bookcases for "tridimensional books," and a twenty-foot container "said to contain 13,770 pounds (net) of carded cotton yarn put up on cones knitting twist waxed with transfer tails." While all this was being loaded and stowed, a tall thin man in gray flannel slacks moved authoritatively among the longshoremen. He would be remembered as the man with the red plastic jug. No one in the crew quite knew who he was, but no one is tracking names or numbers when the ship is aswarm with longshoremen. No one saw the man with the red plastic jug lead three young men up the gangway and under the containers swinging high from cranes. It was just assumed, retrospectively, that that's what he did. The three young men went into an open hatch, and slid into spaces about a foot high on top of the flume tanks (where water is transferred back and forth as an anti-rolling device). When the last of the lollipops had been stowed and lashed, the hatch cover—a huge rectangular steel lid—was secured and the ship was searched, as it always is, for contraband and stowaways. Hatch by hatch, Andy and the chief mate spent thirty minutes searching the hold. Then eight Colombian police-academy cadets, each with a flashlight, went over the same space, searching the ship from bow to stern. Every searcher went past the flume tanks. The police cadets left the ship. The booby hatches (something like manhole covers, and meant for human access to the hold) were dogged and padlocked. The mate wrote in the log: "2200: search conducted in all holds, compartments, lockers, living areas and about the decks for: stowaways, contraband and narcotics; none found." Stella sailed to Panama.

At the dock in Balboa, Peewee and Pope and Victor Belmosa walked up the deck to run a cable to the jumbo crane. They thought they heard a noise of pounding, thumping, somewhere in Port Hatch No. 4. "What's that?" Belmosa said.

Pope said, "The second mate."

Andy was nearby, checking lashings. Belmosa asked him if he had done anything that would cause such a noise.

Andy said he had.

The sailors were about to continue with the cable when the sound came again. Belmosa said, "Did you hear that?"

Andy said he had heard not only a banging sound but also a yell. Andy opened the booby hatch. The three Colombians were just inside it, at the top of a ladder. The temperature in Balboa was not exceptional. It was eighty-seven degrees at the time. The relative humidity was only sixty-four per cent. But the air that came out of the booby hatch could have been rising from a geothermal spring. As the stowaways came out, one of them doubled over with cramps and fell to the deck.

On a transceiver the chief mate called the captain and reported the discovery.

The captain said, "Where are they now, and where were they?"

"They *were* in No. 4."

"Where are they now?"

"They're standing out on deck."

That disquieted the captain. He would have left them in the hatch. From the deck they could jump overboard and swim. He said, "Make sure that they do not get away."

The mate said, "Look, they're dehydrated. They can hardly walk."

The captain said, "That don't make any difference. You put them where they can't get away. If they look like they want to run, I'll be down there with the handcuffs and the gun. They aren't going anywhere."

The stowaways were put in the checker's room, a small space near the top of the gangway where stevedores administer the work of longshoremen. The door, left open a crack, was chained and padlocked. (When the ship is in Port Newark, the checker's room is often filled with longshoremen chattering in Spanish.)

Barring escapes and other complications, the repatriation of the three stowaways would cost Lykes Brothers as much as a hundred thousand dollars. This fact further desensitized whatever tenderness the captain might have felt toward them in memory of his vagabond youth. "They are criminals and I'm the victim," he said. "They have come into our house and caused all kinds of legal problems just like they came in here and stole something. They have illegally entered here, they have trespassed. They may be dehydrated and thirsty and hungry, but when a guy breaks into your house you don't sit him down and treat him with courtesy until the police get there—feed him and water him and tell him that he did good, that you understand that life is tough and he has a perfect right to do this to you. I understand the system from which they flee, but they're criminals and I'm the victim. They've broken a multitude of laws. Ships have been stuck with stowaways for years. You have to be able to identify them. If you don't know where they come from, how are you going to repatriate them? I have to make sure that they don't escape. If they escape into Panama, the thing multiplies. It's our responsibility anyway. It's double our responsibility if they escape."

The three men in the checker's room were still carrying their Colombian citizenship cards, identifying them as Pedro Antonio Moreno Hurtado, Luis Eduardo Mosquera Yepe, and Miguel Enrique Bonilla Sinisterra. They were twenty-seven, twenty-four, and twenty-two years old. The mate went into the No. 4 hold, found the red plastic water jug, and remembered the man in the gray flannel slacks. He had probably sold his services. He was probably a travel agent for stowaways. The mate said regretfully, "I would have bet my home that no one was down there."

Past the chain and padlock, through the slightly open

door, people on the deck could observe the prisoners. One was short and chubby. The others were slim and hawklike. As I peered in, one of them came near and pointed with anguish at his stomach. I asked him if he was sick or just hungry. He said he was hungry and no longer sick.

Scarcely had I turned to ask Andy what might be done about the stowaways' hunger when Victor Belmosa appeared on deck with rolls and bread. In large gulps, the three ate the rolls and the bread. Andy went down to the galley for more bread and a jar of jelly. The port police arrived, with a slogan on their car that said "1995—NOT A STEP BACKWARD." Handcuffed together, the stowaways were taken down the gangway carrying a bag of bread.

Duke Labaczewski said, "My grandfather on my mother's side and my grandfather on my father's side—that's how they came to the United States."

Victor Belmosa looked gently at Duke. Victor had also entered the United States as a nautical stowaway. At the age of seventeen, he had left Trinidad hidden in a Moore-McCormack ship bound for Alabama, he said. Mormac caught him. "A Mormac man in Mobile chewed me out. Then he helped me get a job. That's how I got here."

It could be said of our poor stowaways that they picked the wrong Merchant Marine, for in a sense their presence was betrayed more by the age of the ship than by any other factor. It is less than a day's voyage from Buenaventura to Balboa. I imagine them relatively cool and confident at 4 A.M. that morning, successfully stowed away, feeling the ship's great momentum as a venturous rush, up the dark Pacific. Not far away, in the engine room, David Carter has been checking the pumps, the generators, the air-conditioning. With Karl Knudsen, he has started to transfer fuel oil. He checks the pressures of the gland steam, of the high-pressure steam chest, of the high- and low-pressure bleeds. He checks the temperatures of the bearings (around a hundred and forty-five degrees), the temperature of the desuperheater outlet (five hundred and ninety-five degrees), the temperature of the main steam at the throttle (eight hundred and forty). He and Knudsen change a couple of burners, noticing certain inconsistencies in the fuel-flow apertures, which make no sense to them, so they study the boiler manual. They read it standing together, as if they were sharing a hymnal.

They blow tubes, getting rid of carbon. Blowing tubes is chimney sweeping on a violent scale. Red lights blink on the flame scanners, yellow lights over the burners. Knudsen puts the burners in manual override, so they won't trip out. Otherwise steam could extinguish the flames. If the flames go out, the engine stops. You have lost the plant.

Over the bridge, a cloud of cinders leaves the stack, smudging, for the moment, the diamond colors of Sirius, the bright light of a full Venus. The air clears. The sword of Orion is studded with nebulas. The Pleiades hang like grapes. We have a big papaya on the bridge, and wedges of fresh lemon. This does not tempt Calvin. As an eater, he does not soar above all prejudices. Calvin, at the wheel, looks boneless and destroyed. He is again rest-broken, after another arduous day. Dawn arrives, and Mac, relieving Calvin, comes on angry. While still on the port watches that were set in Buenaventura, the ship sailed in late evening, and sea watches were not restored until midnight. This was a violation of a long nautical tradition: sea watches are set in the first minute of a day of departure, not the last. The core of Mac's complaint is not that he worked eighteen hours and then went on lookout after three hours' sleep. He is used to that. The core of his complaint is that no part of the effort was voluntary. "Your privilege has been taken away," he explains, in a voice loud enough to go through the steel deck. "Setting sea watches *after* you sail. Lord Nelson would roll over in his grave." A slice of papaya helps Mac to calm down. Papaya is alkaline and very soothing. Papaya will pacify an incandescent stomach.

After breakfast, Phil Begin, the chief engineer, stops by the captain's cabin. He is thinking of drawing fuel from the No. 1 After Deep Tank, which has not been used in some time. In Buenaventura, as containers went on and off, there was a net loss of weight in the stern. In one port the bow comes up, in another the stern comes up—a ballasting problem that in part can be corrected by the use of fuel. Because a sloshing tank can be dangerous to a ship, you must generally take all or nothing, and that complicates planning. The capacity of the No. 1 After Deep Tank is thirty-five hundred barrels, or six hundred tons, of fuel. The tank is below the No. 1 hold, at the forward end of the ship. The captain, agreeing, says to Phil Begin, "Thirty-five hundred barrels burned up front will lift the bow eighteen inches and put the stern down six inches."

Within two hours, alarms and sirens are resounding all over the ship. The scent of bunker fuel rises through the house. The lights go out. The stairwells are dark. The rest of the house is in twilight. With a devastating surge, the emergency generator cuts in. It dies. It starts again. Cool, conditioned air rapidly warms. The three-centimetre radar is down, the gyro is nonfunctional, the SatNav is inventing bizarre facts. The steering system is out of control, the rudder irretrievably at hard left. The ship makes an arc in the water as she loses her momentum. The alarms are strident, and they do not stop. What must the stowaways be thinking?

The engineers of the idle watches get out of their bunks and go below. Between the fireroom and the control platform, they crowd the engineers' flat. Engineers famous for doing nothing stand to the side doing nothing. The rest are participants in an orchestrated frenzy, following the orders of the chief. As one and another break from the huddle, they go off running. Begin stays by the throttles. He dispatches his engineers to open valves, close valves, start pumps, stop pumps. They splash through water, ankle deep, that has spilled out of the evaporator. The temperature of the engine room steadily rises, in the absolute humidity of escaping steam.

Very evidently, the burners have gone out because water is in the fuel oil. It is Begin's surmise that a heating coil has sprung a leak. Bunker fuel is somewhat gelatinous and has to be heated to help it move. In various places, it is heated by steam in coils—first in the original tank and then in settling tanks, which in this vessel are near the stern. From the No. 1 After Deep Tank the fuel has travelled five hundred feet to the settling tanks, then two hundred feet back to the burners. The water may be in it anywhere or everywhere. "You don't know you have water in fuel oil until it hits the boiler," Begin says. So the length of his dilemma is seven hundred feet.

The fuel-oil pressure drops to nothing. The fires are out. The emergency diesel generator can supply only a low percentage of the ship's routine electrical demands, and of the blowers that bring fresh air to the engine room only one is working. Every engineer is wetter and hotter than he would be under a shower. As the engineers move, they sway a little. They wonder if they are suffering heatstroke. In David Carter's words, "We are not exactly tense, we just don't want it to get worse. Our adrenaline is up, but Begin knows what he is doing." The coolest places in the engine room now exceed a hundred and fifty degrees. What none of us know is that the rising heat in the No. 4 hold is cooking three stowaways and closing their adventure.

On the bridge deck, in the all but unstirring tropical air, Bill Beach says of the engineers, "This is when they earn their money." He tells of a Dutch ship some hundreds of miles off California at the end of December with no power. Her engine room was flooded. The ship that Beach was on circled the Dutch ship while she waited for an oceangoing tug. For forty-eight consecutive hours, Beach had no sleep as he kept messages passing between the two ships. Finally, he went to bed. While he slept, a message came from the Dutch. Beach was awakened to decipher it. They were saying "Happy New Year."

In the wheelhouse, sitting in his swivel chair and staring forward into a stack of containers, Captain Washburn is talking to himself. "The problem is water," he says. "It doesn't burn well."

As he muses on, his preference for steamships (over the more recent generation of diesels) is not eroding. When a steamship is sinking, the last thing that happens is that seawater going down the stack explodes the boilers, he says.

Otherwise, safety devices are adequate, and boilers don't blow up. Yes, in the Red Sea in 1977 the main crossover from the high-level to the low-pressure turbine on the Waterman ship Robert E. Lee blew itself to pieces, severing lines and pipes and sending shrapnel all over the engine room. The ship had to be towed back to the United States. But, hey, while Washburn was the skipper of the diesel Cygnus the ship lost the plant nineteen times.

What everyone seems to sense but no one specifically knows is that the predicament of the Stella Lykes is far more fundamental than a ruptured coil in a fuel line. As things will turn out, that is not where the water has come from. In Port Newark, an iridescent film afloat beside the ship will lead to an inspection that finds a break in the hull. Our trouble is not as trivial as leaking internal steam. The ship has cracked. And the No. 1 After Deep Tank has cracked with it—admitting from the outside a steady flow of green sea. The captain has been running this old ship slowly—rarely exceeding eighteen knots—to keep her alive, to keep her active, to save her from the breakers, to avoid straining the plant. In the aging atrophy of the Merchant Marine, there is nothing to replace her.

The metal railings on the stairway leading down into the engine room are now much too hot to grip. Gradually, Begin and the others clear the seven hundred feet of pipe. Then, after igniting one burner, they bring one boiler to pressure range. Then they start one turbine, and, in turn, one generator, to send electricity to the main switchboard. Begin describes this as a balancing act. Twice, he loses the balance and has to start again. Hour after hour in the volcanic heat, the work continues.

Meanwhile, from the halyards of the uppermost mast two black balls are flying. Andy calls them "Panamanian running lights." They are six feet apart, and each is not less than two feet in diameter. From two miles away, they are meant to stand out. They look like death lanterns. They punctuate a message. To ships of the world—Liberian, Haitian, Russian, or Greek—they say "Not Under Command."

An impatient albatross circles the bow. Sirens and alarms continue. From under the stern comes an occasional thump, presumably from the rudder. Maybe it's a fish. Duke the bosun has tied a white rag to a 5/0 fishhook and put it over the stern on an orange nylon line of quarter-ton test, hoping for a giant fish. The clouds are very dark off the starboard quarter. With our lemons and lollipops and terry-cloth towels, our three thousand cases of wine, with our ninety drums of passion-fruit juice, our onions, umbrellas, bone glue, and balsa wood, our kiln-dried radiata pine, with our glass Nativity scenes and our peach chips, we are dead in the water.